COOKSHELF

Barbecue

& Salads for Summer

Jacqueline Bellefontaine

This is a Parragon Book
This edition published in 2002
Parragon
Queen Street House
4 Queen Street
Bath BA1 1HE, UK

Hardback ISBN: 0-75254-391-1
Paperback ISBN: 0-75254-139-0

Printed in China

Note

Cup measurements in this book are for American cups. Tablespoons are
assumed to be 15 ml. Unless otherwise stated, milk is assumed to be full fat,
eggs are medium and pepper is freshly ground black pepper.

Contents

Introduction   4

Fish & Seafood   6

Poultry   48

Meat   94

Vegetables & Salads   172

Desserts   234

Index   256

Introduction

What is it that makes a meal cooked outdoors over burning coals so appetizing? Perhaps it's the fresh air or maybe the tantalizing aroma or the sound of fresh food sizzling on the cooking rack. Whatever it is, there is no doubt that barbecues (grills) are becoming more and more popular. This is hardly surprising when you see just how many wonderful dishes can be cooked over charcoal. This book alone contains 120 recipes, leaving you with no shortage of inspiration.

Gone are the days when sausages and burgers were the staple of every barbecue (grill) party, although traditionalists will find recipes here for making fabulous burgers and for tangy sauces to serve with the sausages. But why not try fish, which cooks to perfection on the barbecue (grill) and is healthy too?

There are also dozens of tasty marinades and bastes for meat lovers, as well as vegetarian dishes as alternatives, salads and side dishes. You can even cook a dessert on the barbecue (grill).

WHICH BARBECUE (GRILL)?

You do not need a large, sophisticated barbecue (grill) to produce mouthwatering food, although once you have tried some of these recipes you might want to invest in something larger.

Essentially barbecues (grills) are an open fire with a rack set over the hot coals, on which the food is cooked. You can improvise a makeshift barbecue (grill) with nothing more complicated than a few house bricks and an old oven rack. **Chicken wire** and **baking racks** can also be used to cook on. Purpose-made barbecues (grills) are, however, available in all shapes and sizes, from small disposable trays to large wagon, gas-powered models.

As the names suggest, **portable** and **semi-portable barbecues** (grills) tend to be small. Some types have a stand or folding legs; others have fixed legs. If you have a small model and are cooking for large numbers, cook the food in rotation so that guests can begin on the first course while the second batch is cooking.

Most **brazier barbecues** (grills), which stand on long legs and have a wind shield, are light and portable. On some models the height of the rack can be varied, and some types incorporate rotisseries.

Covered barbecues (grills) are essential if you want to cook whole joints of meat. The lid completely covers the barbecue (grill), increasing the temperature at which food cooks and acting, in effect, like an oven. The temperature is controlled by air vents. When used without the cover, these barbecues (grills) are treated like traditional barbecues (grills).

Wagon barbecues (grills) are larger and more sophisticated. They have wheels and often incorporate a tabletop.

Electric or **gas barbecues** (grills) heat volcanic lava coals. The flavour is still good, because the flavour of barbecued (grilled) food comes from the aromas of its own fat and juices burning on the coals, rather than from the fuel itself.

EQUIPMENT

Apart from the barbecue (grill) itself, you do not need any special equipment, but do arm yourself with a pair of **oven gloves** (potholders). **Long-handled tools** can be useful, as well as being safer and more convenient to use. They are not expensive, and if you cook on a barbecue (grill) regularly it is a good idea to invest in a set. **Racks** for burgers, sausages and fish are useful but not essential.

You will need a set of **skewers** if you want to cook kebabs (kabobs). *Metal skewers* should be flat to stop the food slipping round as it cooks. Remember that metal skewers get very hot, so wear gloves (potholders) or use *tongs* to turn them. *Wooden skewers* are much cheaper than metal skewers but are not always very long lasting. Always soak wooden skewers in cold water for at least 30 minutes before use to help prevent them from burning on the barbecue (grill) and then cover the exposed ends with pieces of kitchen foil.

A **water spray** is useful for cooling down coals or dampening down flare-ups.

LIGHTING THE BARBECUE (GRILL)

Charcoal is the most popular fuel although you can use wood. Charcoal is available as *lump wood*, which is irregular in shape and size but easy to light, or as *briquettes*, which burn for longer and with a more uniform heat; however, they are harder to ignite.

Light the barbecue (grill) at least an hour before you want to start cooking. Stack the coals in the pan and use specially designed solid or liquid lighter fuels to help set the charcoal alight. Do not use household fire lighters because these will taint the food. Never use paraffin or petrol to light a barbecue (grill) – this can be very dangerous.

The barbecue (grill) is ready to use when the flames have completely died down and the coals are covered with a white ash. When the coals are ready, spread them out into a uniform layer.

PREPARING TO COOK

Before you begin to cook, oil the rack so that the food does not stick to it. Do this away from the barbecue (grill) or the oil will flare up as it drips on to the coals. For most dishes, position the rack about 7.5 cm/3 inches above the coals. Raise the rack if you want to slow down the cooking. If you cannot adjust the height of the rack, you can slow down the cooking by spreading out the coals or moving the food to the edges of the rack, where the heat will be less intense.

If your barbecue (grill) has air vents, use them to control the temperature – open the vents for more heat, close them for less.

It is very difficult to give exact times for cooking on a barbecue (grill), so use the times given in the recipes in this book as a guide only. Always test the food to make sure that it is cooked throughly before serving.

5

Fish & Seafood

Fish tastes wonderful when it is cooked on the barbecue (grill). This chapter is full of ideas, ranging from simple char-grilled whole fish to spicy marinated parcels and kebabs (kabobs). Oily fish is especially suitable for the barbecue (grill) because the flesh does not dry out over the direct heat. White fish will benefit from the addition of a baste or marinade if it is cooked directly over the coals, but smaller fish can be cooked whole, because the skin keeps in all the wonderful juices and acts as a natural protective coating. Barbecue (grill) fish steaks with a marinade or baste direct on the rack.

Choose a fish with a firm flesh or it may break up and drop on to the coals when you turn it. Alternatively, a hinged rack will make turning infinitely easier. A firm fish, such as monkfish, is essential for skewers; wrap more delicate fish in kitchen foil, so that it cooks in its own juice.

Seafood is quick to cook and does not need to be left in a marinade for long, making it ideal for impromptu barbecues (grills). Prawn (Shrimp) Skewers, for example, can be made and cooked in minutes.

Indonesian-style Spicy Cod

Serves 4

INGREDIENTS

4 cod steaks
1 stalk lemon grass
1 small red onion, chopped
3 cloves garlic, chopped
2 fresh red chillies, deseeded
    and chopped

1 tsp grated root (fresh)
    ginger
$^1/_4$ tsp turmeric
2 tbsp butter, cut into small
    cubes
8 tbsp canned coconut milk

2 tbsp lemon juice
salt and pepper
red chillies, to garnish
    (optional)

1 Rinse the cod steaks and pat them thoroughly dry on absorbent kitchen paper.

2 Remove and discard the outer leaves from the lemon grass and thinly slice the inner section.

3 Place the lemon grass, onion, garlic, chilli, ginger and turmeric in a food processor and blend until the ingredients are finely chopped. Season with salt and pepper to taste.

4 With the processor running, add the butter, coconut milk and lemon juice and process until well blended.

5 Place the fish in a shallow, non-metallic dish. Pour over the coconut mixture and turn the fish until well coated.

6 If you have one, place the fish steaks in a hinged basket, which will make them easier to turn. Barbecue (grill) over hot coals for 15 minutes or until the fish is cooked through, turning once. Serve garnished with red chillies, if wished.

COOK'S TIP

If you prefer a milder flavour omit the chillies altogether. For a hotter flavour do not remove the seeds from the chillies.

Blackened Fish

Serves 4

INGREDIENTS

4 white fish steaks
1 tbsp paprika
1 tsp dried thyme
1 tsp cayenne pepper

1 tsp freshly ground black
pepper
$^1/_2$ tsp freshly ground white
pepper

$^1/_2$ tsp salt
$^1/_4$ tsp ground allspice
50 g/1$^3/_4$ oz unsalted butter
3 tbsp sunflower oil

1 Rinse the fish steaks and pat them dry with absorbent kitchen paper.

2 Mix together the paprika, thyme, cayenne peppers, black and white peppers, salt and allspice in a shallow dish.

3 Place the butter and oil in a small saucepan and heat, stirring occasionally, until the butter melts.

4 Brush the butter mixture liberally all over the fish steaks, on both sides.

5 Dip the fish into the spicy mix until well coated on both sides.

6 Barbecue (grill) the fish over hot coals for about 10 minutes on each side, turning once. Continue to baste the blackened fish with the remaining butter mixture during the cooking time.

COOK'S TIP

Basting the fish with the butter mixture will ensure that the fish remains moist during cooking.

VARIATION

A whole fish - red mullet, for example - rather than steaks is also delicious cooked this way. The spicy seasoning can also be used to coat chicken portions, if you prefer.

Monkfish Skewers with Courgettes (Zucchini) & Lemon

Serves 4

INGREDIENTS

450 g/1 lb monkfish tail
2 courgettes (zucchini)
1 lemon
12 cherry tomatoes
8 bay leaves

SAUCE:
4 tbsp olive oil
2 tbsp lemon juice
1 tsp chopped, fresh thyme
1/2 tsp lemon pepper

salt

TO SERVE:
green salad leaves
fresh, crusty bread

1 Using a sharp knife, cut the monkfish into 5 cm/2 inch chunks. Cut the courgettes (zucchini) into thick slices and the lemon into wedges.

2 Thread the monkfish, courgettes (zucchini), lemon, tomatoes and bay leaves on to 4 skewers.

3 To make the basting sauce, combine the oil, lemon juice, thyme, lemon pepper and salt to taste in a small bowl.

4 Brush the basting sauce liberally all over the fish, lemon, tomatoes and bay leaves on the skewers.

5 Cook the skewers on the barbecue (grill) for about 15 minutes, basting frequently with the sauce, until the fish is cooked through.

6 Serve the kebabs with green salad leaves and warm, fresh crusty bread.

VARIATION

Use plaice (flounder) fillets instead of the monkfish, if you prefer. Allow two fillets per person, and skin and cut each fillet lengthwise into two. Roll up each piece and thread them on to the skewers.

Monkfish Skewers with Coconut & Coriander (Cilantro)

Serves 4

INGREDIENTS

450 g/1 lb monkfish tails
225 g/8 oz uncooked peeled
    prawns (shrimp)
desiccated (shredded) coconut,
    toasted, to garnish
    (optional)

MARINADE:
1 tsp sunflower oil
$^1/_2$ small onion, finely grated
1 tsp root (fresh) ginger,
    grated

150 ml/5 fl oz/$^2/_3$ cup canned
    coconut milk
2 tbsp chopped, fresh
    coriander (cilantro)

1 To make the marinade, heat the oil in a wok or saucepan and fry the onion and ginger for 5 minutes until just softened but not browned.

2 Add the coconut milk to the pan and bring to the boil. Boil rapidly for about 5 minutes or until reduced to the consistency of single (light) cream.

3 Remove the pan from the heat and allow to cool completely. Once cooled, stir in the coriander (cilantro) and pour into a shallow dish.

4 Cut the fish into bite-sized chunks and stir gently into the coconut mixture with the prawns (shrimp). Chill in the refrigerator for 1–4 hours.

5 Thread the fish and prawns (shrimp) on to skewers and discard any remaining marinade.

Barbecue (grill) over hot coals for 10–15 minutes, turning often. Garnish with toasted coconut.

VARIATION

Look out for uncooked prawns (shrimp) in the freezer cabinet in large supermarkets. If you cannot find them, use cooked prawns (shrimp), but they only need heating through.

Charred Tuna Steaks

Serves 4

INGREDIENTS

4 tuna steaks
3 tbsp soy sauce
1 tbsp Worcestershire sauce
1 tsp wholegrain mustard

1 tsp caster (superfine) sugar
1 tbsp sunflower oil
green salad, to serve

TO GARNISH:
flat-leaf parsley
lemon wedges

1 Place the tuna steaks in a shallow dish.

2 Mix together the soy sauce, Worcestershire sauce, mustard, sugar and oil in a small bowl. Pour the marinade over the tuna steaks.

3 Gently turn over the tuna steaks, using your fingers or a fork, so that they are well coated with the marinade.

4 Cover and place the tuna steaks in the refrigerator and leave to chill for up to 2 hours.

5 Barbecue (grill) the fish over hot coals for 10–15 minutes, turning once. Baste frequently with the marinade.

6 Garnish with flat-leaf parsley and lemon wedges, and serve with a fresh green salad.

COOK'S TIP

Tuna has a dark red flesh, which turns paler on cooking. Tuna has a good meaty texture, but if you are unable to obtain it, use swordfish steaks instead.

COOK'S TIP

If a marinade contains soy sauce, the marinating time should be limited, usually to 2 hours. If allowed to marinate for too long, the fish will dry out and become tough.

Char-grilled Bream

Serves 2

INGREDIENTS

2 small sea bream, scaled, gutted, trimmed and cleaned	BASTE:	TO GARNISH:
2 slices lemon	4 tbsp olive oil	fresh bay leaves
2 bay leaves	2 tbsp lemon juice	fresh thyme sprig
salt and pepper	$^1/_2$ tsp chopped, fresh oregano	lemon wedges
	$^1/_2$ tsp chopped, fresh thyme	

1 Using a sharp knife, cut 2–3 deep slashes into the bodies of both fish in order to help them fully absorb the flavour of the basting sauce.

2 Place a slice of lemon and a bay leaf inside the cavity of each fish. Season inside the cavity with salt and pepper.

3 In a small bowl, mix together the ingredients for the baste using a fork. Alternatively, place the basting ingredients in a small screw-top jar and shake well to combine.

4 Brush some of the baste liberally over the fish and place them on a rack over hot coals. Barbecue (grill) over hot coals for 20-30 minutes, turning and basting frequently.

5 Transfer the fish to a serving plate, garnish with fresh bay leaves, thyme and lemon wedges and serve.

VARIATION

If you prefer, use brill or a fish like gurnand instead of the sea bream.

COOK'S TIP

The flavour of the dish will be enhanced if you use good fresh ingredients in the sauce. Dried herbs can be used, but remember that the flavour is much more intense, so only use half the quantity of the fresh herbs listed above.

Salmon Yakitori

Serves 4

INGREDIENTS

350 g/12 oz chunky salmon fillet 8 baby leeks	YAKITORI SAUCE: 5 tbsp light soy sauce 5 tbsp fish stock 2 tbsp caster (superfine) sugar	5 tbsp dry white wine 3 tbsp sweet sherry 1 clove garlic, crushed

1 Skin the salmon and cut the flesh into 5 cm/2 inch chunks. Trim the leeks and cut them into 5 cm/2 inch lengths.

2 Thread the salmon and leeks alternately on to 8 pre-soaked wooden skewers. Leave to chill in the refrigerator until required.

3 To make the sauce, place all of the ingredients in a small pan and heat gently, stirring, until the sugar dissolves. Bring to the boil, then reduce the heat and simmer for 2 minutes. Strain the sauce and leave to cool.

4 Pour about one-third of the sauce into a small dish and set aside to serve with the kebabs (kabobs).

5 Brush plenty of the remaining sauce over the skewers and cook directly on the rack or, if preferred, place a sheet of oiled kitchen foil on the rack and cook the salmon on that. Barbecue (grill) the skewers over hot coals for about 10 minutes, turning once. Baste frequently during cooking with the remaining sauce to prevent the fish and vegetables from drying out. Serve the kebebs (kabobs) with the reserved sauce for dipping.

COOK'S TIP

Soak the wooden skewers in cold water for at least 30 minutes to prevent them from burning during cooking. You can make the kebabs (kabobs) and sauce several hours before required and refrigerate.

Salmon Brochettes

Serves 4

INGREDIENTS

450 g/1 lb salmon, skinned and cut into large chunks
1 tbsp cornflour (cornstarch)
$^1/_2$ tsp salt
$^1/_2$ tsp pepper
1 small egg white, beaten
1 red (bell) pepper, deseeded and cut into chunks

1 green (bell) pepper, deseeded and cut into chunks
4 tbsp olive oil
ciabatta bread, to serve

TOMATO SAUCE:
4 tomatoes, deseeded and quartered

$^1/_4$ cucumber, peeled, deseeded and chopped
8 basil leaves
6 tbsp olive oil
2 tbsp lemon juice
salt and pepper

1 Place the salmon in a shallow dish and sprinkle over the cornflour (cornstarch), and salt and pepper to taste. Add the beaten egg white and toss well to coat. Leave to chill for 15 minutes.

2 Thread the pieces of salmon on to 4 skewers, alternating the fish pieces with the chunks of red and green (bell) peppers. Set the skewers aside until required.

3 To make the sauce, place all of the ingredients in a food processor and chop coarsely. Alternatively, chop the tomatoes, cucumber and basil leaves by hand and mix with the oil, lemon juice and seasoning. Leave to chill.

4 To serve, barbecue (grill) the salmon brochettes over hot coals for 10 minutes, brushing frequently with olive oil to

prevent them from drying during cooking.

5 Slice the ciabatta bread at an angle to produce 4 long slices. Lightly toast on the barbecue (grill).

6 Spread the sauce over each slice of bread and top with a brochette. You can serve the brochettes on toasted French sticks.

Japanese-style Char-grilled Plaice (Flounder)

Serves 4

INGREDIENTS

4 small plaice (flounders)
6 tbsp soy sauce
2 tbsp sake or dry white wine
2 tbsp sesame oil
1 tbsp lemon juice

2 tbsp light muscovado sugar
1 tsp root (fresh) ginger, grated
1 clove garlic, crushed

TO GARNISH:
1 small carrot
4 spring onions (scallion)

1 Rinse the fish and pat them dry on absorbent kitchen paper. Cut a few slashes into both sides of each fish.

2 Mix together the soy sauce, sake or wine, oil, lemon juice, sugar, ginger and garlic in a large, shallow dish.

3 Place the fish in the marinade and turn so that they are coated on both sides. Chill in the refrigerator for 1–6 hours.

4 Meanwhile, prepare the garnish. Cut the carrot into evenly-sized thin sticks and clean and shred the spring onions (scallions).

5 Barbecue (grill) the fish over hot coals for about 10 minutes, turning the fish once.

6 Scatter the spring onions (scallions) and carrot over the fish and transfer the fish to a serving dish. Serve immediately.

VARIATION

Use sole instead of the plaice (flounders) and scatter over some toasted sesame seeds instead of the carrot and spring onions (scallions), if you prefer.

Smoky Fish Skewers

Serves 4

INGREDIENTS

350 g/12 oz smoked cod fillet	MARINADE:	$^{1}/_{4}$ tsp dried dill
350 g/12 oz cod fillet	4 tbsp sunflower oil	salt and pepper
8 large raw prawns (shrimp)	2 tbsp lemon or lime juice	
8 bay leaves	rind of $^{1}/_{2}$ lemon or lime,	
fresh dill, to garnish (optional)	grated	

1 Skin both types of cod and cut the flesh into bite-size pieces. Peel the prawns (shrimp), leaving just the tail.

2 To make the marinade, combine the sunflower oil, lemon or lime juice, grated lemon or lime rind, dried dill and salt and pepper to taste in a shallow, non-metallic dish.

3 Place the fish in the marinade and stir until the fish is well coated on all sides. Leave to marinate for 1–4 hours.

4 Thread the fish on to 4 skewers, alternating the 2 types of cod with the prawns (shrimp) and bay leaves.

5 Cover the rack with lightly buttered kitchen foil and place the fish skewers on top of the foil.

6 Barbecue (grill) the fish skewers over hot coals for 5-10 minutes, basting with any remaining marinade, turning once.

7 Garnish with fresh dill and serve.

COOK'S TIP

Cod fillet can be rather flaky, so choose the thicker end which is easier to cut into chunky pieces. Line the rack with kitchen foil rather than cooking the fish directly on the rack so that, even if the fish does break away from the skewer, it is not wasted.

Apricot Char-grilled Mackerel

Serves 4

INGREDIENTS

4 mackerel	3 tbsp Worcestershire sauce	dash Tabasco sauce
400 g/14 oz can apricots in natural juice	3 tbsp soy sauce	1 clove garlic, crushed (optional)
3 tbsp dark muscovado sugar	2 tbsp tomato purée (paste)	salt and pepper
	1 tsp ground ginger	

1 Clean and gut the mackerel, removing the heads if preferred. Place the fish in a large, shallow dish.

2 Drain the apricots, reserving the juice. Roughly chop half of the apricots and set aside until required.

3 Place the remaining apricots in a food processor with the sugar, Worcestershire sauce, soy sauce, tomato purée (paste), ginger, Tabasco sauce and garlic (if using) and process until smooth. Alternatively, chop the apricots and mix with the other ingredients.

4 Pour the sauce over the fish, turning them so that they are well coated on both sides. Leave to chill in the refrigerator.

5 Transfer the mackerel to the barbecue (grill) either directly on the rack or on a piece of greased kitchen foil. Barbecue (grill) the mackerel over hot coals for 5–7 minutes, turning once.

6 Spoon any remaining marinade into a saucepan. Add the reserved chopped apricots and about half of the reserved apricot juice and bring to the boil. Reduce the heat and simmer for 2 minutes.

7 Transfer the mackerel to a serving plate and serve with the sauce.

COOK'S TIP

Use a hinged rack if you have one as it will make it much easier to turn the fish during barbecueing (grilling).

Mackerel with Lime & Coriander (Cilantro)

Serves 4

INGREDIENTS

4 small mackerel, trout or
   sardines
1/4 tsp ground coriander
1/4 tsp ground cumin
4 sprigs fresh coriander
   (cilantro)

3 tbsp chopped, fresh
   coriander (cilantro)
1 red chilli, deseeded and
   chopped
grated rind and juice of 1 lime
2 tbsp sunflower oil

salt and pepper
1 lime, sliced, to garnish
chilli flowers, to garnish
   (optional)
salad leaves, to serve

1 To make the chilli flowers (if using), cut the tip of a small chilli lengthwise into thin strips, leaving the chilli intact at the stem end. Remove the seeds and place in iced water until curled.

2 Clean and gut the mackerel, removing the heads if preferred. Place on a chopping board.

3 Sprinkle the fish with the ground spices and salt and pepper to taste. Place a sprig of coriander (cilantro) inside the cavity of each fish.

4 Mix together the chopped coriander (cilantro), chilli, lime rind and juice and the oil in a small bowl. Brush the mixture liberally over the fish.

5 Place the fish in a hinged rack if you have one. Barbecue (grill) the fish over hot coals for 3–4 minutes on each side, turning once. Brush frequently with the remaining basting mixture.

6 Garnish with lime slices and chilli flowers, if using, and serve with salad leaves.

Mediterranean-style Sardines

Serves 4

INGREDIENTS

8–12 fresh sardines
8–12 sprigs of fresh thyme
3 tbsp lemon juice

4 tbsp olive oil
salt and pepper

TO GARNISH:
lemon wedges
tomato slices
fresh herbs

1 Clean and gut the fish if this has not already been done.

2 Remove the scales by rubbing the back of a knife from head to tail along the body. Wash and pat the sardines dry on absorbent kitchen paper.

3 Tuck a sprig of fresh thyme into the body of each sardine. Transfer the sardines to a large, non-metallic dish and season with salt and pepper.

4 Beat together the lemon juice and oil in a bowl and pour the mixture over the sardines. Leave the sardines to marinate in the refrigerator for about 30 minutes.

5 Remove the sardines from the marinade and place them in a hinged basket, if you have one, or on a rack. Barbecue (grill) the sardines over hot coals for 3–4 minutes on each side, basting frequently with any of the remaining marinade.

6 Serve garnished with lemon wedges, tomato slices and fresh herbs.

COOK'S TIP

Look out for small sardines or sprats. Prepare them as above and use the same marinade. Place a piece of greased kitchen foil on the rack and cook over hot coals for 2–3 minutes on each side.

VARIATION

For a slightly different flavour and texture, toss the fish in dried breadcrumbs, then baste with a little olive oil for a crispy coating.

Nutty Stuffed Trout

Serves 4

INGREDIENTS

4 medium trout, cleaned	rind of 1 orange, grated	oil for brushing
2 tbsp sunflower oil	2 tbsp orange juice	salt and pepper
1 small onion, chopped finely	75 g/2³/4 oz fresh wholemeal	orange slices, to garnish
50 g/1³/4 oz toasted mixed	breadcrumbs	orange and watercress salad,
nuts, chopped	1 medium egg, beaten	to serve

1 Season the trout inside and out with salt and pepper to taste.

2 To make the stuffing, heat the oil in a small saucepan and fry the onion until soft. Remove the pan from the heat and stir in the chopped nuts, grated orange rind, orange juice and the breadcrumbs. Add just enough beaten egg to bind the mixture together.

3 Divide the stuffing into 4 equal portions and spoon into the body of each fish.

4 Brush the fish liberally with oil and barbecue (grill) over medium hot coals for 10 minutes on each side, turning once. When the fish is cooked the flesh will be white and firm and the skin will be beginning to crispen.

5 Transfer the fish to individual serving plates and garnish with orange slices.

6 Serve the fish with an orange and watercress salad and an orange and mustard dressing.

COOK'S TIP

Serve the stuffed trout with an orange and watercress salad. For the dressing, mix together 2 tbsp orange juice, 1 tbsp white wine vinegar, 3 tbsp olive oil, ¹/2 tsp wholegrain mustard and salt and pepper to taste. Pour the dressing over the orange and watercress salad just before serving.

Barbecued Herrings with Lemon

Serves 4

INGREDIENTS

4 herrings, cleaned	1 lemon, sliced	1/2 tsp lemon pepper
4 bay leaves	50 g/1 3/4 oz unsalted butter	fresh crusty bread, to serve
salt	2 tbsp chopped, fresh parsley	

1 Season the prepared herrings inside and out with freshly ground salt to taste.

2 Place a bay leaf inside the cavity of each fish.

3 Place 4 squares of kitchen foil on the work surface and divide the lemon slices evenly among them. Place a fish on top of the lemon slices.

4 Beat the butter until softened, then mix in the parsley and lemon pepper. Dot the flavoured butter liberally all over the fish.

5 Wrap the fish tightly in the kitchen foil and barbecue (grill) over medium hot coals for 15-20 minutes or until the fish is cooked through – the flesh should be white in colour and firm to the touch (unwrap the foil to check, then wrap up the fish again).

6 Transfer the wrapped fish parcels to individual, warm serving plates.

7 Unwrap the foil parcels just before serving and serve the fish with fresh, crusty bread to

mop up the deliciously flavoured cooking juices.

VARIATION

For a main course use trout instead of herring. Cook for 20–30 minutes until the flesh is firm to the touch and opaque in colour.

Sardines with Olives & Tomatoes

Serves 4

INGREDIENTS

12 fresh sardines, gutted and
  cleaned
fresh basil leaves
4 plum tomatoes
8 pitted black olives

15 g/^{1}/$_2$ oz butter
1 tbsp olive oil
2 tbsp lemon juice
salt and pepper

TO GARNISH:
plum tomatoes, sliced
olives, sliced
1 fresh basil sprig

1 Season the sardines inside and out with salt and pepper to taste. Insert 1-2 basil leaves inside the cavity of each fish. Using a sharp knife, make a few slashes in the body of each fish.

2 Cut the tomatoes and olives into slices and transfer to a large bowl. Tear 4 basil leaves into small pieces and toss together with the tomatoes and olives.

3 Divide the tomato and olive mixture among

4 large sheets of kitchen foil, and place 3 sardines on top of each portion.

4 Melt the butter and oil in a small pan. Stir in the lemon juice and pour the mixture over the fish.

5 Carefully wrap up the fish in the foil. Barbecue (grill) the fish over medium hot coals for 15–20 minutes until the fish is cooked through.

6 Transfer the fish to individual serving plates and remove the foil.

Garnish the fish with slices of tomato and olive, and with a fresh sprig of basil. Serve at once.

COOK'S TIP

Slashing the body of the fish helps the flesh to absorb the flavours. It is particularly important if you do not have time to allow the fish to marinate before cooking.

Bacon & Scallop Skewers

Makes 4

INGREDIENTS

grated rind and juice of $^1/_2$ lemon	12 scallops	1 yellow (bell) pepper
4 tbsp sunflower oil	1 red (bell) pepper	6 rashers smoked streaky
$^1/_2$ tsp dried dill	1 green (bell) pepper	bacon

1 Mix together the lemon rind and juice, oil and dill in a non-metallic dish. Add the scallops and mix thoroughly to coat in the marinade. Leave to marinate for 1–2 hours.

2 Cut the red, green and yellow (bell) peppers in half and deseed them. Cut the (bell) pepper halves into 2.5 cm/1 inch pieces and then set aside until required.

3 Carefully remove the rind from the bacon. Stretch the bacon rashers with the back of a knife, then cut each bacon rasher in half.

4 Remove the scallops from the marinade, reserving any excess marinade. Wrap a piece of bacon around each scallop.

5 Thread the bacon-wrapped scallops on to skewers, alternating with the (bell) pepper pieces.

6 Barbecue (grill) the bacon and scallop skewers over hot coals for about 5 minutes, basting with the marinade.

7 Transfer the bacon and scallop skewers to serving plates and serve at once.

VARIATION

Peel 4–8 raw prawns (shrimp) and add them to the scallops. Thread them on to the skewers alternately with the scallops and (bell) peppers.

Herrings with
Orange Tarragon Stuffing

Serves 4

INGREDIENTS

1 orange
4 spring onions (scallions)
50 g/1³/4 oz fresh wholemeal
  breadcrumbs
1 tbsp fresh tarragon, chopped

4 herrings, cleaned and gutted
salt and pepper
green salad, to serve

TO GARNISH:
2 oranges
1 tbsp light brown sugar
1 tbsp olive oil
sprigs of fresh tarragon

1 To make the stuffing, grate the rind from half of the orange, using a zester.

2 Peel and chop all of the orange flesh on a plate in order to catch all of the juice.

3 Mix together the orange flesh, juice, rind, spring onions (scallions), breadcrumbs and tarragon in a bowl. Season with salt and pepper to taste.

4 Divide the stuffing into 4 equal portions and use it to fill the body cavities of the fish.

5 Place each fish on to a square of lightly greased kitchen foil and wrap the foil around the fish so that it is completely enclosed. Barbecue (grill) over hot coals for 20–30 minutes until the herrings are cooked through – their flesh should be white and firm to the touch.

6 Meanwhile make the garnish. Peel and thickly slice the 2 oranges and sprinkle over the sugar. Just before the fish is cooked, drizzle a little oil over the orange slices and place them on the barbecue for 5 minutes to heat through.

7 Transfer the fish to serving plates and garnish with the barbecued (grilled) orange slices and sprigs of fresh tarragon. Serve with a green salad.

Caribbean Prawns (Shrimp)

Serves 4

INGREDIENTS

16 cooked king (tiger) prawns
(shrimp)
1 small pineapple
flaked coconut, to garnish
(optional)

MARINADE:
150 ml/5 fl oz/²/₃ cup
pineapple juice
2 tbsp white wine vinegar
2 tbsp dark muscovado sugar

2 tbsp desiccated (shredded)
coconut

1 Peel the prawns
(shrimp), leaving the
tails attached if preferred.

2 Peel the pineapple and
cut it in half
lengthwise. Cut one
pineapple half into wedges
then into chunks.

3 To make the marinade,
mix together half of
the pineapple juice and the
vinegar, sugar and coconut
in a shallow, non-metallic
dish. Add the peeled
prawns (shrimp) and
pineapple chunks and toss
until well coated. Leave to

marinate for at least
30 minutes.

4 Remove the pineapple
and prawns (shrimp)
from the marinade and
thread them on to skewers.
Reserve the marinade.

5 Strain the marinade
and place in a food
processor. Roughly chop
the remaining pineapple
and add to the processor
with the remaining
pineapple juice. Process
the pineapple for a few
seconds to produce a
thick sauce.

6 Pour the sauce into a
small saucepan. Bring
to the boil then simmer for
about 5 minutes.

7 Transfer the kebabs
(kabobs) to the
barbecue (grill) and brush
with some of the sauce.
Barbecue (grill) for about
5 minutes until the kebabs
(kabobs) are piping hot.
Turn the kebabs (kabobs),
brushing occasionally with
the sauce. Serve with extra
sauce, sprinkled with
flaked coconut (if using),
on the side.

Herb & Garlic Prawns (Shrimp)

Serves 4

INGREDIENTS

350 g/12 oz raw prawns (shrimp), peeled	4 tbsp lemon juice	2 cloves garlic, chopped
2 tbsp chopped, fresh parsley	2 tbsp olive oil	salt and pepper
	65 g/2¼ oz butter	

1 Place the prepared prawns (shrimp) in a shallow, non-metallic dish with the parsley, lemon juice and salt and pepper to taste. Leave the prawns (shrimp) to marinate in the herb mixture for at least 30 minutes.

2 Heat the oil and butter in a small pan with the garlic until the butter melts. Stir to mix thoroughly.

3 Remove the prawns (shrimp) from the marinade with a perforated spoon and add them to the pan containing the garlic butter. Stir the prawns (shrimp) into the garlic butter until well coated, then thread the prawns (shrimp) on to skewers.

4 Barbecue (grill) the kebabs (kabobs) over hot coals for 5–10 minutes, turning the skewers occasionally, until the prawns (shrimp) turn pink and are cooked through. Brush the prawns (shrimp) with the remaining garlic butter during the cooking time.

5 Transfer the herb and garlic prawn (shrimp) kebabs (kabobs) to serving plates. Drizzle over any of the remaining garlic butter and serve at once.

VARIATION

If raw prawns (shrimp) are unavailable, use cooked prawns (shrimp) but reduce the cooking time. Small cooked prawns (shrimp) can also be cooked in a kitchen foil parcel istead of on the skewers. Marinate and toss the cooked prawns (shrimp) in the garlic butter, wrap in kitchen foil and cook for about 5 minutes, shaking the parcels once or twice.

Poultry

Poultry can be cooked in a number of ways on the barbecue (grill). Try it with herbs and garlic, tangy tomato glazes or spicy oriental flavours. It also goes well with sweet glazes and fruit.

Chicken is ideal, because the skin helps to keep the flesh succulent and gives a crispy coating. It is essential that all poultry is cooked thoroughly. Test by piercing with a skewer in the thickest part – the juices should run clear when the meat is cooked. To avoid charred skins and raw centres, cook over coals that are not too hot. Place the rack about 10 cm/ 4 inches above the coals. You should be able to hold your hand just above the rack for about 5 seconds; if it is too hot reduce the temperature by raising the rack or spreading out the coals. However if the coals are not hot enough, the chicken will take too long to cook and will dry out.

Turkey can be a little dry, so baste it frequently with a glaze or marinade. Duckling has a stronger flavour and more fat than chicken or turkey. Larger joints of poultry can be parcooked in boiling water, the oven or microwave and finished on the barbecue (grill).

Jerk Chicken

Serves 4

INGREDIENTS

4 chicken portions
1 bunch spring onions
   (scallions), trimmed
1–2 Scotch Bonnet chillies,
   deseeded
1 garlic clove

5 cm/2 inch piece root (fresh)
   ginger, peeled and roughly
   chopped
$1/2$ tsp dried thyme
$1/2$ tsp paprika
$1/4$ tsp ground allspice

pinch ground cinnamon
pinch ground cloves
4 tbsp white wine vinegar
3 tbsp light soy sauce
pepper

1 Rinse the chicken portions and pat them dry on absorbent kitchen paper. Place them in a shallow dish.

2 Place the spring onions (scallions), chillies, garlic, ginger, thyme, paprika, allspice, cinnamon, cloves, wine vinegar, soy sauce and pepper to taste in a food processor and process to make a smooth mixture.

3 Pour the spicy mixture over the chicken. Turn the chicken portions over so that they are well coated in the marinade. Transfer the chicken to the refrigerator and leave to marinate for up to 24 hours.

4 Remove the chicken from the marinade and barbecue (grill) over medium hot coals for about 30 minutes, turning the chicken over and basting occasionally with any remaining marinade, until the chicken is cooked through.

5 Transfer the chicken portions to individual serving plates and serve at once.

COOK'S TIP

As Jamaican cuisine becomes increasingly popular, you will find jars of ready-made jerk marinade, which you can use when time is short. Allow the chicken to marinate for as long as possible for maximum flavour.

Favourite Barbecued (Grilled) Chicken

Serves 4

INGREDIENTS

8 chicken wings or 1 chicken cut into 8 portions	3 tbsp brown fruity sauce	1 tbsp olive oil
3 tbsp tomato purée (paste)	1 tbsp white wine vinegar	1 clove garlic, crushed (optional)
	1 tbsp clear honey	salad leaves, to serve

1 Remove the skin from the chicken if you want to reduce the fat in the dish.

2 To make the barbecue glaze, place the tomato purée (paste), brown fruity sauce, white wine vinegar, honey, oil and garlic in a small bowl. Stir all of the ingredients together until they are thoroughly blended.

3 Brush the barbecue (grill) glaze over the chicken and barbecue (grill) over hot coals for 15–20 minutes. Turn the chicken portions over occasionally and baste frequently with the barbecue (grill) glaze. If the chicken begins to blacken before it is cooked, raise the rack if possible or move the chicken to a cooler part of the barbecue (grill) to slow down the cooking.

4 Transfer the barbecued (grilled) chicken to warm serving plates and serve with a selection of fresh salad leaves.

VARIATION

This barbecue (grill) glaze also makes a very good baste to brush over pork chops.

COOK'S TIP

When poultry is cooked over a very hot barbecue (grill) the heat immediately seals in all of the juices, leaving the meat succulent. For this reason you must make sure that the coals are hot enough before starting to barbecue (grill).

Sticky Chicken Drumsticks

Serves 10

INGREDIENTS

10 chicken drumsticks	1 tbsp Worcestershire sauce	TO SERVE:
4 tbsp fine-cut orange	grated rind and juice of	cherry tomatoes
marmalade	$^{1}/_{2}$ orange	salad leaves
	salt and pepper	

1 Using a sharp knife, make 2–3 slashes in the flesh of each chicken drumstick.

2 Bring a large saucepan of water to the boil and add the chicken drumsticks. Cover the pan, return to the boil and cook for 5–10 minutes. Remove the chicken and drain thoroughly.

3 Meanwhile, make the baste. Place the orange marmalade, Worcestershire sauce, orange rind and juice and salt and pepper to taste in a small saucepan.

Heat gently, stirring continuously, until the marmalade melts and all of the ingredients are well combined.

4 Brush the baste over the par-cooked chicken drumsticks and transfer them to the barbecue (grill) to complete cooking. Barbecue (grill) over hot coals for about 10 minutes, turning and basting frequently with the remaining baste.

5 Carefully thread 3 cherry tomatoes on to a skewer and transfer to

the barbecue (grill) for 1–2 minutes.

6 Transfer the chicken drumsticks to serving plates. Serve with the cherry tomato skewers and a selection of fresh salad leaves.

COOK'S TIP

Par-cooking the chicken is an ideal way of making sure that it is cooked through without becoming overcooked and burned on the outside.

Chicken Tikka

Makes 6

INGREDIENTS

4 chicken breasts, skinned and
boned
$\frac{1}{2}$ tsp salt
4 tbsp lemon or lime juice

MARINADE:
150 ml/5 fl oz/$\frac{2}{3}$ cup natural
yogurt

2 cloves garlic, crushed
2.5 cm/1 inch piece root
(fresh) ginger, peeled and
grated
1 tsp ground cumin
1 tsp chilli powder
$\frac{1}{2}$ tsp ground coriander
$\frac{1}{2}$ tsp ground turmeric

oil or melted butter for
brushing

SAUCE:
150 ml/5 fl oz/ $\frac{2}{3}$ cup natural
yogurt
1 tsp mint sauce

1 Cut the chicken into
2.5 cm/1 inch cubes.
Sprinkle with the salt and
the lemon or lime juice
and leave to stand for about
10 minutes.

2 To make the marinade,
combine the yogurt,
garlic, ginger and ground
spices together in a small
bowl until well mixed.

3 Thread the chicken
cubes on to skewers
and brush with the

marinade. Cover and
leave to marinate in the
refrigerator for at least 2
hours, preferably overnight.

4 Barbecue (grill) the
chicken skewers over
hot coals, brushing with oil
or butter and turning
frequently, for about
15 minutes or until cooked
through.

5 Meanwhile, combine
the yogurt and mint to
make the sauce. Serve the

chicken skewers with the
mint and yogurt sauce.

VARIATION

*Use the marinade to coat
chicken portions, such as
drumsticks, rather than
cubes of chicken, if you
prefer. Barbecue (grill) over
medium hot coals for
30–40 minutes, until the
juices run clear when the
chicken is pierced
with a skewer.*

Indian Charred Chicken

Serves 4

INGREDIENTS

4 chicken breasts, skinned and boned
2 tbsp curry paste
1 tbsp sunflower oil
1 tbsp light muscovado sugar
1 tsp ground ginger

$^1/_2$ tsp ground cumin

TO SERVE:
naan bread
green salad leaves

CUCUMBER RAITA:
$^1/_4$ cucumber
salt
150 ml/5 fl oz/$^2/_3$ cup natural yogurt
$^1/_4$ tsp chilli powder

1 Place the chicken breasts between sheets of baking parchment or cling film (plastic wrap). Pound them with the flat side of a meat mallet or rolling pin to flatten them.

2 Mix together the curry paste, oil, sugar, ginger and cumin in a small bowl. Spread the mixture over both sides of the chicken and set aside until required.

3 To make the raita, peel the cucumber and scoop out the seeds with a spoon. Grate the cucumber flesh, sprinkle with salt, place in a sieve and leave to stand for 10 minutes. Rinse off the salt and squeeze out any moisture by pressing the cucumber with the base of a glass or back of a spoon.

4 Mix the cucumber with the yogurt and stir in the chilli powder. Leave to chill in the refrigerator until required.

5 Transfer the chicken to an oiled rack and barbecue (grill) over hot coals for 10 minutes, turning once.

6 Warm the naan bread at the side of the barbecue. Serve the chicken with the naan bread and raita and accompanied with fresh green salad leaves.

COOK'S TIP

Flattening the chicken breasts makes them thinner so that they cook more quickly.

Cajun Spicy Chicken

Serves 4

INGREDIENTS

4 chicken portions
1 clove garlic
1 tbsp light muscovado sugar
3 tbsp paprika

2 tsp cayenne pepper
1 tsp dried oregano
1 tsp dried sage
1 tsp dried thyme

4 tbsp sunflower oil
2 tbsp lemon juice
salt and pepper

1 Remove the skin from the chicken if you want to reduce the fat content of this recipe. Using a sharp knife, make 2–3 slashes in the flesh of the chicken.

2 Cut the garlic clove in half and rub the cut surface over the chicken. Season the chicken portions with salt and pepper to taste.

3 Mix together the sugar, spices and dried herbs in a small bowl. Sprinkle over the chicken and rub into the flesh. Cover and leave to stand for at least 2 hours.

4 Mix together the oil and lemon juice in a small bowl. Brush the mixture liberally over the chicken.

5 Barbecue (grill) the chicken over medium hot coals for about 30 minutes, turning and basting occasionally with the oil and lemon mixture.

6 Check that the chicken is cooked by piercing the thickest part with a skewer – the juices should run clear. Return the chicken to the barbecue (grill) to cook for a little longer if necessary.

7 Transfer the chicken to warm serving plates and serve at once.

VARIATION

This recipe also works well with pork. Rub the spiced mixture on to pork chops or belly pork slices – they will taste delicious.

Spatchcock Baby Chicken with Garlic & Herbs

Serves 2

INGREDIENTS

2 baby chickens, each
    450 g/1lb
75 g/2³⁄4 oz butter
2 cloves garlic, crushed

2 tbsp chopped, mixed fresh
herbs

BASTE:
4 tbsp olive oil
2 tbsp lemon juice
2 tbsp chopped, mixed herbs
salt and pepper

1 To spatchcock each chicken, place each bird on its breast and use sharp scissors or poultry shears to cut along the length of the back bone. Open out the bird as much as possible and place it breast-side up on a chopping board. Press down firmly on the breast bone to break it.

2 Mix together the butter, garlic and herbs until well combined. Lift up the skin from the breast of each chicken. Divide the butter equally between the 2 chickens and spread over the breast under the skin.

3 Open out each bird. Thread 2 skewers diagonally through each bird to hold it flat.

4 Mix together the ingredients for the baste in a bowl.

5 Place the birds, bone-side down, over medium hot coals and barbecue (grill) for 25 minutes, basting with the lemon and herb baste. Turn the birds over and barbecue (grill), skin-side down, for 15 minutes, basting frequently, or until cooked through.

COOK'S TIP

Use fresh herbs: thyme, rosemary, mint, oregano, parsley or coriander (cilantro) are all suitable.

Sweet Maple Chicken

Serves 6

INGREDIENTS

2 boned chicken thighs
5 tbsp maple syrup
1 tbsp caster (superfine) sugar
grated rind and juice of
¹/₂ orange
2 tbsp tomato ketchup

2 tsp Worcestershire sauce

TO GARNISH:
slices of orange
sprig of flat-leaf parsley

TO SERVE:
focaccia bread
salad leaves
cherry tomatoes, quartered

1 Using a sharp knife, make 2–3 slashes in the flesh of the chicken. Place the chicken in a shallow, non-metallic dish.

2 To make the marinade, mix together the maple syrup, sugar, orange rind and juice, ketchup and Worcestershire sauce.

3 Pour the marinade over the chicken, tossing the chicken to coat thoroughly. Cover and leave to chill in the refrigerator until required.

4 Remove the chicken from the marinade, reserving the marinade for basting.

5 Transfer the chicken to the barbecue (grill) and cook over hot coals for 20 minutes, turning and basting with the marinade.

6 Transfer the chicken to serving plates and garnish with slices of orange and a sprig of fresh-leaf parsley. Serve with focaccia bread, fresh salad leaves and cherry tomatoes.

COOK'S TIP

If time is short you can omit the marinating time. If you use chicken quarters, rather than the smaller thigh portions, par-boil them for 10 minutes before brushing with the marinade and barbecueing (grilling).

Chicken Skewers with Lemon & Coriander (Cilantro)

Serves 4

INGREDIENTS

4 chicken breasts, skinned and boned
1 tsp ground coriander
2 tsp lemon juice

300 ml/¹/₂ pint/1¹/₄ cups natural yogurt
1 lemon

2 tbsp chopped, fresh coriander (cilantro)
oil for brushing
salt and pepper

1 Cut the chicken into 2.5 cm/1 inch pieces and place them in a shallow, non-metallic dish.

2 Add the coriander, lemon juice, salt and pepper to taste and 4 tbsp of the yogurt to the chicken and mix together until thoroughly combined. Cover and leave to chill for at least 2 hours, preferably overnight.

3 To make the lemon yogurt, peel and finely chop the lemon, discarding any pips. Stir the lemon into the yogurt, with the fresh coriander (cilantro). Chill in the refrigerator.

4 Thread the chicken pieces on to skewers. Brush the rack with oil and barbecue (grill) over hot coals for about 15 minutes, basting with the oil.

5 Transfer the kebabs (kabobs) to warm serving plates and garnish with coriander (cilantro), lemon wedges and salad leaves. Serve with yogurt.

VARIATION

These kebabs (kabobs) are delicious served on a bed of blanched spinach, which has been seasoned with salt, pepper and nutmeg.

COOK'S TIP

Prepare the chicken the day before it is needed so that it can marinate overnight.

Chicken Satay

Serves 4

INGREDIENTS

2 chicken breasts, skinned and
    boned

MARINADE:
4 tbsp sunflower oil
2 cloves garlic, crushed
3 tbsp fresh, chopped
    coriander (cilantro)
1 tbsp caster (superfine) sugar

¹/₂ tsp ground cumin
¹/₂ tsp ground coriander
1 tbsp soy sauce
1 red or green chilli, deseeded
salt and pepper

SAUCE:
2 tbsp sunflower oil
1 small onion, chopped finely

1 red or green chilli, deseeded
    and chopped
¹/₂ tsp ground coriander
¹/₂ tsp ground cumin
8 tbsp peanut butter
8 tbsp chicken stock or water
1 tbsp block coconut

1 Soak 8 wooden skewers in a large, shallow dish of cold water for at least 30 minutes. This will prevent the skewers from burning on the hot grill.

2 Cut the chicken lengthwise into 8 long strips. Thread the strips of chicken, concertina-style, on to the skewers and set them aside while you make the marinade.

3 Place the ingredients for the marinade in a food processor and process until smooth.

4 Coat the chicken with the marinade paste, cover and leave to chill in the refrigerator for at least 2 hours.

5 To make the sauce, heat the oil in a small pan and fry the onion and chilli until they are softened but not browned. Stir in the spices and cook for 1 minute. Add the remaining sauce ingredients and cook the mixture gently for 5 minutes. Keep warm.

6 Barbecue (grill) the chicken skewers over hot coals for about 10 minutes, basting with any remaining marinade. Serve immediately with the warm sauce.

Thai-style Chicken Skewers

Serves 4

INGREDIENTS

4 chicken breasts, skinned and
  boned
1 onion, peeled and cut into
  wedges
1 large red (bell) pepper,
  deseeded

1 large yellow (bell) pepper
  deseeded
12 kaffir lime leaves
2 tbsp sunflower oil
2 tbsp lime juice
tomato halves, to serve

MARINADE:
1 tbsp Thai red curry paste
150 ml/5 fl oz/$^2/_3$ cup canned
  coconut milk

1 To make the marinade, place the red curry paste in a small saucepan over a medium heat and cook for 1 minute. Add half of the coconut milk to the saucepan and bring the mixture to the boil. Boil gently for 2–3 minutes until the liquid has reduced by about two-thirds.

2 Remove the saucepan from the heat and stir in the remaining coconut milk. Set the mixture aside to cool.

3 Cut the chicken into 2.5 cm/1 inch pieces. Stir the chicken into the cold marinade, cover and leave to chill for at least 2 hours.

4 Cut the onion into wedges and the (bell) peppers into 2.5 cm/1 inch pieces.

5 Remove the chicken pieces from the marinade and thread them on to skewers, alternating the chicken with the vegetables and lime leaves.

6 Combine the oil and lime juice in a small bowl and brush the mixture over the kebabs (kabobs). Barbecue (grill) the skewers over hot coals, turning and basting for 10–15 minutes until the chicken is cooked through. Barbecue (grill) the tomato halves and serve with the chicken skewers.

Sesame Chicken Brochettes with Cranberry Sauce

Makes 8

INGREDIENTS

4 chicken breasts, skinned and boned
4 tbsp dry white wine
1 tbsp light muscovado sugar
2 tbsp sunflower oil
100 g/3$^1/_2$ oz sesame seeds

salt and pepper

TO SERVE:
boiled new potatoes
green salad leaves

SAUCE:
175 g/6 oz cranberries
150 ml/5 fl oz/$^2/_3$ cup cranberry juice drink
2 tbsp light muscovado sugar

1 Cut the chicken into 2.5 cm/1 inch pieces. Put the wine, sugar, oil and salt and pepper to taste in a large bowl, stirring to combine. Add the chicken pieces and toss to coat. Leave to marinate for at least 30 minutes, turning the chicken occasionally.

2 To make the sauce, place the ingredients in a small saucepan and bring slowly to the boil, stirring. Simmer gently for

5–10 minutes until the cranberries are soft and pulpy. Taste and add a little extra sugar if wished. Keep warm or leave to chill.

3 Remove the chicken pieces from the marinade with a perforated spoon. Thread the chicken pieces on to 8 skewers, spacing them slightly apart to ensure even cooking.

4 Barbecue (grill) on an oiled rack over hot

coals for 4–5 minutes on each side until just cooked. Brush several times with the marinade.

5 Remove the chicken skewers from the rack and roll in the sesame seeds. Return to the barbecue (grill) and cook for about 1 minute on each side or until the sesame seeds are toasted.Serve with the cranberry sauce, new potatoes and green salad leaves.

Chicken Skewers with Red (Bell) Pepper Sauce

Serves 4

INGREDIENTS

3 chicken breasts, skinned and
    boned
6 tbsp olive oil
4 tbsp lemon juice
$1/2$ small onion, grated
1 tbsp fresh, chopped sage
8 tbsp sage and onion stuffing
    mix

6 tbsp boiling water
2 green (bell) peppers,
    deseeded

SAUCE:
1 tbsp olive oil
1 red (bell) pepper, deseeded
    and chopped finely

1 small onion, chopped finely
pinch sugar
210 g/$7^1/2$ oz can chopped
    tomatoes

1 Cut the chicken into evenly sized pieces. Mix the oil, lemon juice, grated onion and sage and pour into a polythene bag. Add the chicken, seal and shake. Marinate for 30 minutes, shaking occasionally. Place the stuffing mix in a bowl and add the boiling water, stirring well.

2 Cut each (bell) pepper into 6 strips, then blanch in boiling water for 3–4 minutes. Drain and refresh under running water, then drain again.

3 Form about 1 tsp of the stuffing mixture into a ball and roll it up in a strip of (bell) pepper. Repeat for the remaining stuffing mixture and (bell) pepper strips. Thread 3 rolls on to each skewer alternately with pieces of chicken. Chill.

4 To make the sauce, heat the oil in a small pan and fry the (bell) pepper and onion for 5 minutes. Add the sugar and tomatoes and simmer for 5 minutes. Set aside and keep warm.

5 Barbecue (grill) the skewers on an oiled rack over hot coals, basting frequently, for 15 minutes. Serve with the sauce.

1

2

3

Maryland Chicken Kebabs (Kabobs)

Makes 4

INGREDIENTS

8 chicken thighs, skinned and
    boned
1 tbsp white wine vinegar
1 tbsp lemon juice, plus extra
    for brushing
1 tbsp golden syrup or honey

6 tbsp olive oil
1 clove garlic, crushed
4 rashers rindless, smoked,
    streaky bacon
2 bananas
salt and pepper

TO SERVE:
4 cooked corn-on-the-cobs
    (see page 198)
mango chutney (relish)

1 Cut the chicken into bite-size pieces. Combine the vinegar, lemon juice, syrup or honey, oil, garlic and salt and pepper to taste in a large bowl. Add the chicken to the marinade and toss until well coated. Cover and leave to marinate for 1–2 hours.

2 Stretch the bacon rashers with the back of a knife and then cut each bacon rasher in half. Cut the bananas into 2.5 cm/ 1 inch lengths and brush them with lemon juice to prevent any discoloration.

3 Wrap a piece of bacon around each piece of banana.

4 Remove the chicken from the marinade, reserving the marinade for basting. Thread the chicken pieces and the bacon and banana rolls alternately on to skewers.

5 Barbecue (grill) the kebabs (kabobs) over hot coals for 8–10 minutes until the chicken is completely cooked. Baste the kebabs (kabobs) with the marinade and turn the skewers frequently. Serve with corn-on-the-cobs and mango chutney (relish).

VARIATION

For a quick Maryland-style dish, omit the marinating time and cook the chicken thighs over hot coals for about 20 minutes, basting with the marinade.

3

4

5

Turkey Steaks with Redcurrant Glaze

Serves 4

INGREDIENTS

100 g / 3 1/2 oz redcurrant jelly
2 tbsp lime juice
4 tbsp olive oil
2 tbsp dry white wine
1/4 tsp ground ginger

pinch grated nutmeg
4 turkey breast steaks
salt and pepper

TO SERVE:
mixed salad leaves
vinaigrette dressing
1 ciabatta loaf
cherry tomatoes

1 Put the redcurrant jelly and lime juice in a small pan and heat gently, stirring, until the jelly melts. Stir in the oil, wine, ginger and nutmeg.

2 Place the turkey steaks in a shallow, non-metallic dish and season with salt and pepper. Pour over the redcurrant mixture, turning the meat so that it is well coated. Cover and leave to chill in the refrigerator overnight.

3 Remove the turkey from the marinade,

reserving the marinade for basting, and barbecue (grill) on an oiled rack over hot coals for about 4 minutes on each side. Baste the turkey steaks frequently with the reserved marinade.

4 Meanwhile, toss the salad leaves in the vinaigrette dressing. Cut the ciabatta loaf in half lengthwise and place, cut-side down, at the side of the barbecue. Barbecue (grill) until golden.

5 Cut each piece of bread into 4. Serve the turkey

steaks on top of a salad leaf and sandwiched between 2 pieces of bread.

VARIATION

Turkey and chicken escalopes are also ideal for cooking on the barbecue (grill). Because they are thin, they cook through without burning on the outside. Leave them overnight in a marinade of your choice or cook, basting with a little lemon juice and oil mixture, and season well.

Char-grilled Turkey with Cheesy Pockets

Serves 4

INGREDIENTS

4 turkey breast pieces, each about 225 g/8 oz

4 portions full-fat cheese (Bel Paese, grated Mozzarella or Brie or Camembert), 15 g/^{1}/2 oz each

4 sage leaves or ^{1}/2 tsp dried sage

8 rashers rindless streaky bacon

4 tbsp olive oil

2 tbsp lemon juice

salt and pepper

TO SERVE:
garlic bread
salad leaves
cherry tomatoes

1 Carefully cut a pocket into the side of each turkey breast with a sharp knife. Open out each breast a little and season inside with salt and pepper to taste.

2 Place a portion of cheese into each pocket, spreading it a little with a knife. Tuck a sage leaf into each pocket, or sprinkle the cheese in the pocket with a little dried sage if you prefer.

3 Stretch the bacon out with the back of a knife. Wrap 2 pieces of bacon around each turkey breast, so that the pocket opening is completely covered. You can use a cocktail stick to keep the turkey and bacon in place.

4 Mix together the oil and lemon juice in a small bowl.

5 Barbecue (grill) the turkey over medium hot coals for about 10 minutes on each side, basting with the oil and lemon mixture frequently.

6 Place the garlic bread at the side of the barbecue (grill) and toast lightly.

7 Transfer the turkey to warm serving plates. Serve with the toasted garlic bread, fresh salad leaves and a few cherry tomatoes.

Spicy Turkey & Sausage Kebabs (Kabobs)

Makes 8

INGREDIENTS

turkey breast fillet, about
350 g/12 oz
300 g/10¹/2 oz chorizo
(seasoned pork) sausage
1 dessert (eating) apple

1 tbsp lemon juice
8 bay leaves

BASTE:
6 tbsp olive oil

2 cloves garlic, crushed
1 red chilli, deseeded and
chopped
salt and pepper

1 To make the baste, place the oil, garlic, chilli and salt and pepper to taste in a small screw-top jar and shake well to combine. Leave to stand for 1 hour for the garlic and chilli to flavour the oil.

2 Cut the turkey into 2.5 cm/1 inch pieces. Cut the sausage into 2.5 cm/1 inch lengths.

3 Cut the apple into chunks and remove the core. Toss the apple in lemon juice to prevent discoloration.

4 Thread the turkey and sausage pieces on to 8 skewers, alternating with the apple chunks and bay leaves.

5 Barbecue (grill) the kebabs (kabobs) over hot coals for about 15 minutes or until the turkey is cooked. Turn and baste the kebabs (kabobs) frequently with the flavoured oil.

6 Transfer the kebabs (kabobs) to warm serving plates and serve at once.

COOK'S TIP

The flavoured oil used in this recipe can be used to baste any grilled (broiled) meat, fish or vegetables. It will give plain foods a subtle chilli flavour and will keep in the refrigerator for about 2 weeks.

Sherried Chicken Liver Brochettes

Serves 4

INGREDIENTS

400 g/14 oz chicken liver,
  trimmed and cleaned
3 slices rindless, streaky bacon
1 ciabatta loaf or small French
  stick
225 g/8 oz baby spinach,
  washed

MARINADE:
150 ml/5 fl oz/²/3 cup dry
  sherry
4 tbsp olive oil
1 tsp wholegrain mustard
salt and pepper

MUSTARD MAYONNAISE:
8 tbsp mayonnaise
1 tsp wholegrain mustard

1 Cut the chicken liver into 5 cm/2 inch pieces. To make the marinade, combine the sherry, oil, mustard and salt and pepper to taste in a shallow dish. Add the chicken liver to the marinade and toss until well coated. Leave to marinate for 3–4 hours.

2 To make the mayonnaise, stir the mustard into the mayonnaise and leave to chill.

3 Stretch out the bacon with the back of a knife and cut each slice into 2. Remove the chicken liver from the marinade, reserving the marinade for basting. Wrap the bacon around half of the chicken liver pieces. Thread the bacon and chicken liver rolls and the plain chicken liver pieces alternately on to 6 pre-soaked wooden skewers.

4 Barbecue (grill) the skewers over hot coals for 10-12 minutes, turning and basting with the reserved marinade frequently.

5 Meanwhile, cut the bread into 6 pieces and toast the cut sides on the barbecue (grill) until golden brown.

6 Top the toasted bread with spinach leaves and place the kebabs (kabobs) on top. Spoon over the mayonnaise and serve immediately.

Citrus Duckling Skewers

Serves 12

INGREDIENTS

3 duckling breasts, skinned
  and boned
1 small red onion, cut into
  wedges
1 small aubergine (eggplant),
  cut into cubes

lime and lemon wedges, to
  garnish (optional)

MARINADE:
grated rind and juice of
  1 lemon
grated rind and juice of 1 lime

grated rind and juice of
  1 orange
1 clove garlic, crushed
1 tsp dried oregano
2 tbsp olive oil
dash of Tabasco sauce

1 Cut the duckling into
  bite-size pieces and
place them in a non-
metallic bowl together with
the prepared red onion and
aubergine (eggplant).

2 For the marinade, place
  the lemon, lime and
orange rinds and juices,
garlic, oregano, oil and
Tabasco sauce in a screw-top
jar and shake until mixed.

3 Pour the marinade
  over the duckling and
vegetables and toss to coat.

Leave to marinate for
30 minutes.

4 Remove the duckling
  and vegetables from
the marinade, reserving the
marinade for basting, and
thread them on to skewers.

5 Barbecue (grill) the
  skewers on an oiled
rack over medium hot
coals, turning and basting
frequently with the
reserved marinade, for
15-20 minutes until the
meat is cooked through.

6 Serve the kebabs
  (kabobs) garnished
with lemon and lime
wedges for squeezing,
if using.

COOK'S TIP

*For more zing add 1 tsp of
chilli sauce to the marinade.
The meat can be marinated
for several hours, but
marinate the vegetables for
only 30 minutes.*

Sesame Orange Duckling

Serves 4

INGREDIENTS

4 tbsp soy sauce
2 tbsp fine-cut marmalade
2 tbsp orange juice
2 cloves garlic, crushed

1 cm/^{1}/2 inch piece root
　(fresh) ginger, grated
1 tbsp sherry vinegar
4 duckling portions
2 oranges, sliced

4 tbsp sesame seeds

TO SERVE:
green salad leaves
fresh herbs

1 Mix together the soy sauce, marmalade, orange juice, garlic, ginger and vinegar in a small bowl until well combined.

2 Trim away any excess fat from the duckling portions. Place the duckling portions in a shallow, non-metallic dish and pour over the orange mixture. Cover and leave for at least 2 hours.

3 Divide most of the orange slices among 4 double-thickness pieces of kitchen foil, reserving some orange slices to serve. Place a duckling portion on top of the oranges and pour some of the marinade over each portion. Fold over the foil to enclose the duckling completely.

4 Barbecue (grill) over hot coals for about 40 minutes or until the meat is just cooked.

5 Remove the foil parcels from the heat and sprinkle the skin of the duckling with the sesame seeds. Place the duckling, skin-side down, directly on the oiled rack over the hot coals and barbecue (grill) for a further 5 minutes until the skin is crisp. Serve with the orange slices, salad leaves and fresh herbs.

COOK'S TIP

Cooking the duckling in foil parcels retains all the flavour of the marinade. If you prefer, you can omit the foil and cook them directly on the rack. Turn and baste frequently.

Barbecued (Grilled) Duckling

Serves 4

INGREDIENTS

3 cloves garlic, crushed
150 ml/5 fl oz/²/3 cup light
   soy sauce
5 tbsp light muscovado sugar

2.5 cm/1 inch piece root
   (fresh) ginger, grated
1 tbsp chopped, fresh
   coriander (cilantro)
1 tsp five-spice powder

4 duckling breasts
sprig of fresh coriander
   (cilantro), to garnish

1 To make the marinade, mix together the garlic, soy sauce, sugar, grated ginger, chopped coriander (cilantro) and five-spice powder in a small bowl until well combined.

2 Place the duckling breasts in a shallow, non-metallic dish and pour over the marinade. Carefully turn over the duckling so that it is fully coated with the marinade on both sides.

3 Cover the bowl with cling film (plastic wrap) and leave to marinate for 1-6 hours, turning the duckling once or twice so the marinade is absorbed.

4 Remove the duckling from the marinade, reserving the marinade for basting.

5 Barbecue (grill) the duckling over hot coals for 20–30 minutes, turning the breasts frequently and basting with the reserved marinade.

6 Cut the duckling into slices and transfer to warm serving plates. Serve garnished with a sprig of fresh coriander (cilantro).

COOK'S TIP

Duckling is quite a fatty meat so there is no need to add oil to the marinade. However, you must remember to oil the barbecue (grill) rack to prevent the duckling from sticking. Do this well away from the barbecue (grill) to avoid any danger of a flare-up.

Glazed Duckling with Pineapple Salsa

Serves 4

INGREDIENTS

2 tbsp Dijon mustard
1 tsp paprika
1/2 tsp ground ginger
1/2 tsp ground nutmeg
2 tbsp dark muscovado sugar
2 duckling halves

salad leaves, to serve

SALSA:
225 g/8 oz can pineapple in
    natural juice
2 tbsp dark muscovado sugar

1 small red onion, chopped
    finely
1 red chilli, deseeded and
    chopped

1 To make the salsa, drain the pineapple, reserving 2 tbsp of the juice. Finely chop the pineapple flesh.

2 Place the pineapple, reserved juice, sugar, onion and chilli in a bowl and mix well. Leave to stand for at least 1 hour for the flavours to fully develop.

3 Meanwhile, mix together the mustard,

paprika, ginger, nutmeg and sugar. Spread the mixture evenly over the skin of the duckling halves.

4 Barbecue (grill) the duckling, skin-side up, over hot coals for about 30 minutes. Turn the duckling over and barbecue (grill) for 10–15 minutes or until the duckling is cooked through.

5 Serve with fresh salad leaves and the salsa.

COOK'S TIP

You could place the ducklings in a rectangular foil tray to protect the delicate flesh on the barbecue (grill).

VARIATION

Use canned apricots or peaches to make the salsa for a tasty alternative. The salsa is also delicious served with pork, lamb or chicken.

Meat

Most people think of meat when they think of barbecues (grills), and even the simplest chop tastes wonderful when cooked on the barbecue (grill). Add marinades or bastes, and you have the most appetizing meal you can imagine.

The following recipes include suggestions for all of your favourite cuts of meat, as well as new approaches to those barbecue (grill) favourites, burgers and sausages. Your only problem will be in deciding what not to cook. Don't be afraid of experimenting and mixing the bastes and marinades with different cuts and types of meat.

If you are having an impromptu barbecue (grill) choose recipes with a baste, although if time permits marinating meat not only adds flavour but helps to ensure that the meat is tender. Trim any excess fat from the meat so that it does not drip on to the coals, causing them to flare up – keep a water spray handy just in case.

Beef and lamb can be served pink in the centre, but you must make sure that pork is cooked thoroughly. Test it with a skewer to see if the juices run clear.

Beef Toppers

Makes 6

INGREDIENTS

700 g/1 lb 9 oz minced lean
 beef
1 onion, chopped finely
2 tbsp Worcestershire sauce
salt and pepper
sesame baps, toasted, to serve

SAVOURY MUSHROOMS:
125 g/4 ^{1}/2 oz button
 mushrooms, sliced
1 tbsp soy sauce
1 tbsp Worcestershire sauce

GUACAMOLE:
1 avocado
1 clove garlic

1 tbsp lemon juice
1 tbsp tomato relish

BARBECUE SAUCE:
3 tbsp brown fruity sauce
3 tbsp tomato ketchup
 (catsup)
1 tsp wholegrain mustard
1 tbsp clear honey

1 Choose one or all of the following toppings. To make the savoury mushrooms, combine all of the ingredients together and leave the mixture to marinate for at least 30 minutes.

2 To make the guacamole topping, peel, stone and mash the avocado. Mix the avocado with the garlic, lemon juice and tomato relish and leave to chill in the refrigerator until required.

3 To make the barbecue sauce, combine all of the ingredients together and leave to chill in the refrigerator until required.

4 To make the beefburgers, mix together the minced beef, onion, Worcestershire sauce and salt and pepper to taste until well combined.

Divide into 6 portions and pat each into a neat round, about 1 cm/^{1}/2 inch thick. Leave to chill for at least 30 minutes.

5 Barbecue (grill) over hot coals for 5–10 minutes on each side. Serve the burgers in the baps, with the topping spooned on top.

Beef Teriyaki

Serves 4

INGREDIENTS

450 g/1 lb extra thin beef
    steaks
8 spring onions (scallions),
    trimmed and cut into short
    lengths

1 yellow (bell) pepper,
    deseeded and cut into
    chunks
green salad, to serve

SAUCE:
1 tsp cornflour (cornstarch)

2 tbsp dry sherry
2 tbsp white wine vinegar
3 tbsp soy sauce
1 tbsp dark muscovado sugar
1 clove garlic, crushed
1/2 tsp ground cinnamon
1/2 tsp ground ginger

1 Place the meat in a shallow, non-metallic dish. To make the sauce, combine the cornflour (cornstarch) with the sherry, then stir in the remaining sauce ingredients. Pour the sauce over the meat and leave to marinate for at least 2 hours.

2 Remove the marinated meat from the sauce and set aside. Pour the sauce into a small saucepan.

3 Cut the meat into thin strips and thread these, concertina-style, on to pre-soaked wooden skewers, alternating each strip of meat with the prepared pieces of (bell) pepper and spring onion (scallion).

4 Gently heat the sauce until it is just simmering, stirring occasionally. Barbecue (grill) the kebabs (kabobs) over hot coals for 5–8 minutes, turning and basting the beef and

vegetables occasionally with the reserved sauce.

5 Arrange the skewers on serving plates and pour the remaining sauce over the kebabs (kabobs). Serve with a green salad.

COOK'S TIP

If you are short of time, omit the marinating, but the flavour will not permeate the meat as well.

Boozy Beef Steaks

Serves 4

INGREDIENTS

4 beef steaks	pepper	TO SERVE:
4 tbsp whisky or brandy	fresh sprig of parsley, to	garlic bread
2 tbsp soy sauce	garnish	slices of tomato
1 tbsp dark muscovado sugar		

1 Make a few cuts in the edge of fat on each steak. This will stop the meat curling as it cooks.

2 Place the meat in a shallow, non-metallic dish. Combine the whisky or brandy, soy sauce, sugar and pepper to taste in a small bowl, stirring until the sugar dissolves. Pour the mixture over the steak. Cover and marinate for at least 2 hours.

3 Barbecue (grill) the meat over hot coals, searing the meat over the hottest part of the barbecue (grill) for about 2 minutes on each side.

4 Move the meat to an area with slightly less intense heat and cook for a further 4–10 minutes on each side, depending on how well done you like your steaks. Test the meat is cooked by inserting the tip of a knife into the meat – the juices will run from red when the meat is still rare, to clear as it becomes well cooked.

5 Lightly barbecue (grill) the slices of tomato for 1–2 minutes.

6 Transfer the meat and the tomatoes to warm serving plates. Garnish with a sprig of fresh parsley and serve with garlic bread.

COOK'S TIP

Choose a good quality steak, such as fillet, rump, T-bone or entrecôte, with a light marbling of fat to prevent the meat from becoming too dry as it cooks. Quick-fry steaks can also be used, but these have to be pounded with a meat mallet to flatten and tenderize the meat.

Mexican Steaks with Avocado Salsa

Serves 4

INGREDIENTS

4 beef steaks
3 tbsp sunflower oil
$^1/_2$ red onion, grated
1 red chilli, deseeded and
    chopped finely
1 clove garlic, crushed
1 tbsp chopped, fresh
    coriander (cilantro)

$^1/_2$ tsp dried oregano
1 tsp ground cumin

AVOCADO SALSA:
1 ripe avocado
grated rind and juice of 1 lime
1 tbsp sunflower oil
$^1/_2$ red onion, chopped finely

1 red chilli, deseeded and
    chopped finely
1 tbsp chopped, fresh
    coriander (cilantro)
salt and pepper

1 Make a few cuts in the edge of fat around each steak to prevent the meat from curling as it cooks. Place the meat in a shallow, non-metallic dish.

2 Combine the oil, onion, chilli, garlic, coriander (cilantro), oregano and cumin in a small bowl. Pour the marinade over the steaks, turning the meat so that it is well coated. Leave to marinate for 1–2 hours.

3 To make the salsa, halve the avocado and remove the stone. Peel and cut the flesh into small dice. Combine the avocado with the lime rind and juice, oil, onion, chilli, coriander (cilantro) and salt and pepper to taste and mix well. Cover and leave to chill in the refrigerator .

4 Barbecue (grill) the steaks on an oiled rack over hot coals for 6–12 minutes on each side.

5 Serve with the avocado salsa.

VARIATION

The avocado salsa can also be served with chicken. Reduce the amount of chilli if you want a milder flavour. If fresh chillies are not available, look out for jars of minced chillies, which are a good substitute.

Barbecue Steaks with Red Onion Marmalade

Serves 4

INGREDIENTS

4 rump steaks
2 tsp wholegrain mustard
2 tbsp sunflower oil
grated rind and juice of $^1/_2$
    orange
salt and pepper

cooked new potatoes, to serve

RED ONION MARMALADE:
2 tbsp olive oil
450 g/1 lb red onions, cut into
    rings

200 ml/7 fl oz/$^3/_4$ cup red
    wine
rind of 1 orange, grated
1 tbsp caster (superfine) sugar

1 To make the marmalade, place the olive oil and onions in a saucepan and sauté gently for 5–10 minutes until the onions are just softened and are beginning to turn golden-brown.

2 Add the wine, orange rind and sugar to the pan and simmer for 10–15 minutes until the onions are tender and most of the liquid has evaporated. Leave to cool, then season.

3 Make a few cuts in the edge of fat around each steak to prevent the meat from curling as it cooks.

4 Using a knife, spread each steak with a little of the mustard and season with salt and pepper.

5 Mix together the oil and the orange juice and rind in a small bowl, and use this mixture to baste the steaks occasionally during cooking.

6 Barbecue (grill) the steaks over hot coals, searing the meat over the hottest part for 2 minutes on each side, basting occasionally with the orange mixture. Move the meat to an area with slightly less intense heat and cook, basting occasionally, for 4–10 minutes on each side, depending on how well done you like your steaks. Serve with the marmalade and new potatoes.

Surf & Turf Kebabs (Kabobs)

Makes 6

INGREDIENTS

450 g/1 lb rump or sirloin
 steak
18 raw prawns (shrimp)

MARINADE:
5 tbsp oyster sauce
1 tbsp soy sauce

3 tbsp lemon juice
4 tbsp sunflower oil

1 Cut the steaks into 24 evenly-sized pieces and place the meat in a non-metallic dish.

2 Peel the prawns (shrimp), leaving the tail attached, as these look attractive.

3 To make the marinade, combine the oyster sauce, soy sauce, lemon juice and sunflower oil in a small bowl. Pour the mixture over the meat and leave to marinate for 15 minutes.

4 Add the prawns (shrimp) to the marinade, toss to coat, and let marinate for 5 minutes.

5 Remove the meat and prawns from the marinade, reserving the marinade for basting. Thread the meat on to metal or pre-soaked wooden skewers, alternating the steak with the prawns (shrimp). (Pre-soaking wooden skewers helps to prevent them from burning as the meat cooks.)

6 Barbecue (grill) the kebabs (kabobs) over hot coals for 5–10 minutes, basting with the marinade and turning frequently.

7 Transfer the kebabs (kabobs) to warm serving plates.

VARIATION

Other shellfish, such as lobster and crab, can be added to the skewers. These kebabs (kabobs) are also delicious marinated in, and basted with, a herb, garlic and oil marinade.

Beef, Tomato & Olive Kebabs (Kabobs)

Serves 8

INGREDIENTS

450 g/1 lb rump or sirloin
  steak
16 cherry tomatoes
16 large green olives, pitted
focaccia bread, to serve

BASTE:
4 tbsp olive oil

1 tbsp sherry vinegar
1 clove garlic, crushed
salt and freshly ground black
  pepper

FRESH TOMATO RELISH:
1 tbsp olive oil
1/2 red onion, chopped finely

1 clove garlic, chopped
6 plum tomatoes, deseeded,
  skinned and chopped
2 pitted green olives, sliced
1 tbsp chopped, fresh parsley
1 tbsp lemon juice

1 Trim any fat from the beef and cut the meat into 24 evenly-sized pieces.

2 Thread the meat on to 8 skewers, alternating the meat with cherry tomatoes and olives.

3 To make the baste, combine the oil, vinegar, garlic and salt and pepper to taste in a bowl.

4 To make the relish, heat the oil in a small pan and fry the onion and garlic for 3–4 minutes until softened. Add the tomatoes and olives and cook for 2–3 minutes until the tomatoes are slightly soft. Stir in the parsley and lemon juice and season with salt and pepper to taste. Set aside and keep warm or leave to chill.

5 Barbecue (grill) the skewers on an oiled rack over hot coals for 5–10 minutes, basting and turning frequently. Serve with the tomato relish and slices of focaccia.

COOK'S TIP

The kebabs (kabobs), baste and relish can be prepared several hours in advance, to avoid any last-minute rush. For a simple meal, serve with crusty fresh bread and a mixed salad.

Beef with Wild Mushrooms

Serves 4

INGREDIENTS

4 steaks, fillet or sirloin	150 g/5 1/2 oz mixed wild	TO SERVE:
50 g/1 3/4 oz butter	mushrooms	salad leaves
1–2 cloves garlic, crushed	2 tbsp chopped, fresh parsley	cherry tomatoes, halved

1 Place the steaks on to a chopping board and using a sharp knife, cut a pocket into the side of each steak.

2 To make the stuffing, heat the butter in a frying pan, add the garlic and fry gently for about 1 minute.

3 Add the mushrooms to the pan and sauté gently for 4–6 minutes until tender. Stir in the chopped parsley.

4 Divide the mushroom mixture into 4 and insert a portion into the

pocket of each steak. Seal the pocket closed with a cocktail stick (toothpick). If preparing this recipe in advance, allow the mixture to cool before stuffing the steaks.

5 Barbecue (grill) the steaks over hot coals, searing the meat over the hottest part of the barbecue (grill) for about 2 minutes on each side. Move the steaks to an area with slightly less intense heat and barbecue (grill) for a further 4–10 minutes on each side, depending on how well done you like your steaks.

6 Transfer the steaks to serving plates and remove the cocktail sticks (toothpicks). Serve with salad leaves and cherry tomatoes.

COOK'S TIP

Wild mushrooms, such as shiitake, oyster and chanterelle, are now readily available in supermarkets. Look out for boxes of mixed wild mushrooms, which are usually cheaper than buying the different types individually.

Meatball Brochettes

Makes 8

INGREDIENTS

25 g/1 oz cracked wheat
350 g/12 oz lean minced beef
1 onion, chopped very finely
(optional)

1 tbsp tomato ketchup
(catsup)
1 tbsp brown fruity sauce
1 tbsp chopped, fresh parsley
beaten egg, to bind

8 cherry tomatoes
8 button mushrooms
oil, to baste
8 bread finger rolls, to serve

1 Place the cracked wheat in a bowl and cover with boiling water. Leave to soak for 20 minutes or until softened. Drain thoroughly and leave to cool.

2 Place the wheat, minced beef, onion (if using), ketchup (catsup), brown sauce and parsley together in a mixing bowl and mix well. Add a little beaten egg if necessary to bind the mixture together.

3 Using your hands, shape the meat

mixture into 18 even-sized balls. Leave to chill in the refrigerator for 30 minutes.

4 Thread the meatballs on to 8 pre-soaked wooden skewers, alternating them with the cherry tomatoes and button mushrooms.

5 Brush the kebabs (kabobs) with a little oil and barbecue (grill) over hot coals for about 10 minutes, turning occasionally and brushing with a little more oil if necessary.

6 Transfer the kebabs (kabobs) to warm serving plates. Cut open the bread finger rolls and push the meat and vegetables off the skewer into the open rolls to serve, if you wish.

COOK'S TIP

The cracked wheat 'stretches' the beef, making this a cheap and cheerful meal. It also produces a less dense meatball with a nutty texture that children often like.

Char-grilled Venison Steaks

Serves 4

INGREDIENTS

4 venison steaks
150 ml/5 fl oz/^{2}/$_3$ cup red
   wine
2 tbsp sunflower oil
1 tbsp red wine vinegar
1 onion, chopped

few sprigs fresh parsley
2 sprigs fresh thyme
1 bay leaf
1 tsp caster (superfine) sugar
^{1}/$_2$ tsp mild mustard

salt and pepper

TO SERVE:
jacket potatoes
salad leaves and cherry
   tomatoes

1 Place the venison steaks in a shallow, non-metallic dish.

2 Combine the wine, oil, wine vinegar, onion, fresh parsley, thyme, bay leaf, sugar, mustard and salt and pepper to taste in a screw-top jar and shake vigorously until well combined. Alternatively, using a fork, whisk the ingredients together in a bowl.

3 Pour the marinade mixture over the venison, cover and leave to marinate in the refrigerator overnight. Turn the steaks over in the mixture occasionally so that the meat is well coated.

4 Barbecue (grill) the venison over hot coals, searing the meat over the hottest part of the barbecue (grill) for about 2 minutes on each side.

5 Move the meat to an area with slightly less intense heat and barbecue (grill) for a further 4–10 minutes on each side, depending on how well done you like your steaks. Test if the meat is cooked by inserting the tip of a knife into the meat – the juices will run from red when the meat is still rare to clear as the meat becomes well cooked.

6 Serve with jacket potatoes, salad leaves and tomatoes.

Lamb Burgers with Mint & Pine Nuts

Serves 4

INGREDIENTS

450 g/1 lb lean minced lamb
1 small onion, chopped finely
50 g/1³/4 oz pine nuts

2 tbsp chopped, fresh mint
salt and pepper

TO SERVE:
4 pitta breads or soft baps
75 g/2 ³/4oz Feta cheese
salad leaves

1 Place the minced lamb, chopped onion, pine nuts, fresh mint and salt and pepper to taste in a large bowl and mix together until thoroughly combined.

2 Using your hands, divide the meat mixture into 4 and shape the portions into round burgers, pressing the mixture together well. Cover the portions and leave to chill in the refrigerator for about 30 minutes.

3 Barbecue (grill) the burgers over hot coals for 4–5 minutes on each side, turning once, until the juices run clear.

4 Warm the pitta breads at the side of the barbecue or toast the baps.

5 Crumble the Feta cheese into small pieces and set aside until required.

6 Line the pitta bread or baps with the salad leaves. Sandwich the burgers between the pitta bread or baps, and top with the crumbled Feta cheese.

COOK'S TIP

If you do not have any fresh mint, use 1–2 teaspoons of mint sauce, which has a much fresher taste than dried mint. Leave the burgers to chill in the refrigerator before cooking them so that they become firmer and are far less likely to fall apart.

Butterfly Chops with Redcurrant Glaze

Serves 4

INGREDIENTS

4 tbsp redcurrant jelly
2 tbsp raspberry vinegar
1/2 tsp dried rosemary
1 clove garlic, crushed

1 tbsp sunflower oil
4 butterfly lamb chops or 8
    loin lamb chops

4 baby aubergines (eggplant)
oil, to baste

1 To make the glaze, combine the redcurrant jelly, vinegar, rosemary, garlic and oil in a small pan and heat, stirring occasionally, until the jelly melts and the ingredients are well blended.

2 Barbecue (grill) the chops over hot coals for 5 minutes on each side.

3 Cut each aubergine (eggplant) in half and brush the cut sides liberally with oil.

4 Barbecue (grill) the aubergine (eggplant) alongside the lamb for 3–4 minutes on each side or until cooked through. Set aside and keep warm.

5 Brush the glaze over the chops and barbecue (grill) the meat for a further 5 minutes on each side, basting frequently, until the meat is cooked. Keep the redcurrant glaze warm at the side of the barbecue (grill).

6 Transfer to warm serving plates and pour over the remaining redcurrant glaze. Serve immediately.

VARIATION

You can use other lamb cuts for this dish – leg steaks or chump chops are ideal. The redcurrant glaze also goes well with chicken; par-boil or microwave chicken drumsticks, then brush them with the redcurrant glaze and finish off on the barbecue (grill).

Lamb with a Spice Crust

Serves 4

INGREDIENTS

1 tbsp olive oil
2 tbsp light muscovado sugar
2 tbsp wholegrain mustard

1 tbsp horseradish sauce
1 tbsp plain (all-purpose) flour
350 g/12 oz neck fillet of lamb
salt and pepper

TO SERVE:
coleslaw
slices of tomato

1 Combine the olive oil, muscovado sugar, wholegrain mustard, horseradish sauce, flour and salt and pepper to taste in a shallow, non-metallic dish until they are well combined.

2 Roll the lamb in the spice mixture until well coated.

3 Lightly oil one or two pieces of foil or a large, double thickness of foil. Place the lamb on the foil and wrap it up so that the meat is completely enclosed.

4 Place the foil parcel over hot coals for 30 minutes, turning the parcel over occasionally.

5 Open the kitchen foil, spoon the cooking juices over the lamb and continue to barbecue (grill) for a further 10-15 minutes or until cooked through.

6 Transfer the lamb to a warm serving plate and remove the foil. Cut the lamb into thick slices and serve with coleslaw and a few slices of tomato.

COOK'S TIP

Lamb is naturally fatter than beef, which makes it a good choice for cooking on the barbecue (grill).

COOK'S TIP

If preferred, the lamb can be completely removed from the kitchen foil for the second part of the cooking. Barbecue (grill) the lamb directly over the coals for a smokier barbecue (grill) flavour, basting with extra oil if necessary.

Kibbeh

Makes 8

INGREDIENTS

75 g/2³/₄ oz couscous
1 small onion
350 g/12 oz lean minced lamb
¹/₂ tsp ground cinnamon

¹/₄ tsp cayenne pepper
4 tsp ground allspice
green salad and onion rings,
   to serve

BASTE:
2 tbsp sunflower oil
2 tbsp tomato ketchup
   (catsup)

1 Place the couscous in a large bowl, cover with cold water and leave to stand for 30 minutes or until the couscous has swelled and softened. Alternatively, soak the couscous according to the instructions on the packet.

2 Drain the couscous through a sieve and squeeze out as much moisture as you can.

3 If you have a food processor, add the onion and chop finely. Add the lamb and process briefly to chop the mince further. If you do not have a processor, grate the onion before mixing with the lamb.

4 Combine the couscous, lamb and spices and mix. Divide the mixture into 8 equal sized portions. Press and shape the mixture around 8 skewers, pressing the mixture together firmly so that it holds its shape. Chill for 30 minutes.

5 To make the baste, combine the oil and ketchup (catsup).

6 Barbecue (grill) the kibbeh over hot coals for 10–15 minutes, turning and basting frequently. Serve with barbecued (grilled) onion rings and green salad leaves.

COOK'S TIP

Adding couscous to a mince mixture 'stretches' the meat, making the dish very economical to make. You can add it to other types of mince and use it to make kebabs (kabobs) or burgers.

Barbecued (Grilled) Lamb Ribs

Serves 4

INGREDIENTS

breast of lamb, about 700 g/1
    lb 9 oz
3 tbsp sweet chutney (relish)
4 tbsp tomato ketchup
    (catsup)

2 tbsp cider vinegar
2 tsp Worcestershire sauce
2 tsp mild mustard
1 tbsp light muscovado sugar

TO SERVE:
salad leaves
cherry tomatoes

1 Using a sharp knife, cut between the ribs of the breast of lamb to divide it into slightly smaller pieces.

2 Bring a large saucepan of water to the boil, add the lamb and par-cook for about 5 minutes. Remove the meat from the water and pat dry thoroughly with paper towels.

3 Combine the sweet chutney (relish), tomato ketchup (catsup), cider vinegar,

Worcestershire sauce, mustard and sugar in a shallow, non-metallic dish to make a sauce.

4 Using a sharp knife, cut the lamb into individual ribs. Add the ribs to the sauce and toss until well coated.

5 Remove the ribs from the sauce, reserving the remaining sauce for basting.

6 Barbecue (grill) the ribs over hot coals for 10-15 minutes, turning and

basting frequently with the reserved sauce.

7 Transfer the ribs to warm serving plates. Serve immediately with salad leaves and cherry tomatoes.

VARIATION

Use pork belly strips if you prefer and, as with the lamb, par-cook the pork to remove some of the excess fat from the meat.

Butterfly Lamb with Balsamic Vinegar & Mint

Serves 4

INGREDIENTS

boned leg of lamb, about 1.8 kg/4 lb	150 ml/5 fl oz/²/₃ cup sunflower oil	salt and pepper
8 tbsp balsamic vinegar	4 tbsp chopped, fresh mint	TO SERVE:
grated rind and juice of 1 lemon	2 cloves garlic, crushed	grilled (broiled) vegetables
	2 tbsp light muscovado sugar	green salad leaves

1 Open out the boned leg of lamb so that its shape resembles a butterfly. Thread 2–3 skewers through the meat.

2 Combine the balsamic vinegar, lemon rind and juice, oil, mint, garlic, sugar and salt and pepper to taste in a non-metallic dish that is large enough to hold the lamb.

3 Place the lamb in the dish and turn it over a few times so that the meat is coated on both sides with the marinade. Leave to marinate for at least 6 hours or preferably overnight, turning occasionally.

4 Remove the lamb from the marinade and reserve the liquid.

5 Place the rack about 15 cm/6 inches above the coals and barbecue (grill) the lamb for about 30 minutes on each side, turning once and basting frequently.

6 Transfer the lamb to a chopping board and remove the skewers. Cut the lamb into slices across the grain and serve with grilled (broiled) vegetables and green salad leaves.

COOK'S TIP

If you prefer, cook the lamb for half the cooking time in a preheated oven at 180°C/350°F/Gas Mark 4, then finish off on the barbecue (grill).

Red Wine Lamb Skewers

Makes 4

INGREDIENTS

450 g/1 lb lean lamb
12 button onions or shallots
12 button mushrooms
salad leaves and cherry
    tomatoes, to serve

MARINADE:
150 ml/5 fl oz/^{2}/$_3$ cup red
    wine
4 tbsp olive oil
2 tbsp brandy (optional)

1 onion, sliced
1 bay leaf
sprig of fresh thyme
2 sprigs fresh parsley

1 Carefully trim away any excess fat from the lamb. Cut the lamb into large pieces.

2 To make the marinade, combine the wine, oil, brandy (if using), onion, bay leaf, thyme and parsley in a non-metallic dish.

3 Add the meat to the dish and toss to coat the meat thoroughly in the marinade. Cover the dish and leave to marinate in the refrigerator for at least 2 hours or preferably overnight.

4 Bring a saucepan of water to a rolling boil, drop in the unpeeled button onions and blanch them for 3 minutes. Drain and refresh the onions under cold water, and then drain again. Trim the onions and remove their skins, which will now slip off easily.

5 Remove the meat from the marinade, reserving the liquid for basting. Thread the meat on to skewers, alternating with the button onions and mushrooms.

6 Barbecue (grill) the kebabs (kabobs) over hot coals for 8–10 minutes, turning and basting the meat and vegetables with the reserved marinade a few times.

7 Transfer the lamb kebabs (kabobs) to a warm serving plate and serve with fresh salad leaves and cherry tomatoes.

Moroccan Lamb Kebabs (Kabobs)

Makes 4

INGREDIENTS

450 g/1 lb lean lamb
1 lemon
1 red onion
4 small courgettes (zucchini)
couscous, to serve (see Cook's
Tip)

MARINADE:
grated rind and juice of
1 lemon
2 tbsp olive oil
1 clove garlic, crushed
1 red chilli, sliced (optional)

1 tsp ground cinnamon
1 tsp ground ginger
$1/2$ tsp ground cumin
$1/2$ tsp ground coriander

1 Cut the lamb into large, evenly-sized chunks.

2 To make the marinade, combine the lemon rind and juice, oil, garlic, chilli (if using), ground cinnamon, ginger, cumin and coriander in a large non-metallic dish.

3 Add the meat to the marinade, tossing to coat the meat completely. Cover and leave to marinate in the refrigerator for at least 2 hours.

4 Cut the lemon into 8 pieces. Cut the onion into wedges, then separate each wedge into 2 pieces.

5 Using a canelle knife (or potato peeler), cut thin strips of peel from the courgettes (zucchini), then cut them into chunks.

6 Remove the meat from the marinade, reserving the liquid for basting. Thread the meat on to skewers alternating with the onion, lemon and courgette (zucchini).

7 Barbecue (grill) over hot coals for 8–10 minutes, basting with the reserved marinade.

COOK'S TIP

Serve these kebabs (kabobs) with couscous or tabouleh. Soak the couscous in cold water for about 20 minutes until the grains have softened. Then drain and steam them for 10 minutes or until piping hot.

Shish Kebabs (Kabobs)

Makes 4

INGREDIENTS

450 g/1 lb lean lamb
1 red onion, cut into wedges
1 green (bell) pepper, deseeded

MARINADE:
1 onion

4 tbsp olive oil
grated rind and juice of
$^1/_2$ lemon
1 clove garlic, crushed
$^1/_2$ tsp dried oregano
$^1/_2$tsp dried thyme

TO SERVE:
4 pitta breads
few crisp lettuce leaves,
shredded
2 tomatoes, sliced
chilli sauce (optional)

1 Cut the lamb into large, evenly-sized chunks.

2 To make the marinade, grate the onion or chop it very finely in a food processor. Remove the juice by squeezing the onion between two plates set over a small bowl.

3 Combine the onion juice with the remaining marinade ingredients in a non-metallic dish and add the meat. Toss the meat in the

marinade, cover and leave to marinate in the refrigerator for at least 2 hours or overnight.

4 Divide the onion wedges into 2. Cut the (bell) peppers into chunks.

5 Remove the meat from the marinade, reserving the liquid for basting. Thread the meat on to skewers, alternating with the onion and (bell) peppers. Barbecue (grill) for 8–10 minutes, turning and basting frequently.

6 Split open the pitta breads and fill with a little lettuce, and the meat and vegetables. Top with tomatoes and chilli sauce.

VARIATION

These kebabs (kabobs) are delicious served with saffron-flavoured rice. For easy saffron rice, simply use saffron stock cubes when cooking the rice.

Lamb Cutlets with Rosemary

Serves 4

INGREDIENTS

8 lamb cutlets
5 tbsp olive oil
2 tbsp lemon juice
1 clove garlic, crushed
1/2 tsp lemon pepper
salt
8 sprigs rosemary

jacket potatoes, to serve

SALAD:
4 tomatoes, sliced
4 spring onions (scallion),
    sliced diagonally

DRESSING:
2 tbsp olive oil
1 tbsp lemon juice
1 clove garlic, chopped
1/4 tsp fresh rosemary,
    chopped finely

1 Trim the lamb chops by cutting away the flesh with a sharp knife to expose the tips of the bones.

2 Place the oil, lemon juice garlic, lemon pepper and salt in a shallow, non-metallic dish and whisk with a fork to combine.

3 Lay the sprigs of rosemary in the dish and place the lamb on top. Leave to marinate for at least 1 hour, turning the lamb cutlets once.

4 Remove the chops from the marinade and wrap a little kitchen foil around the bones to stop them from burning.

5 Place the sprigs of rosemary on the rack and place the lamb on top. Barbecue (grill) for 10–15 minutes, turning once.

6 Meanwhile make the salad and dressing.

Arrange the tomatoes on a serving dish and scatter the spring onions (scallions) on top. Place all the ingredients for the dressing in a screw-top jar, shake well and pour over the salad. Serve with the barbecued (grilled) lamb cutlets and jacket potatoes.

Lamb with Mango & Chilli

Serves 4

INGREDIENTS

4 chump lamb chops
4 tbsp mango chutney (relish)
2 tsp chilli sauce
grilled vegetables, to serve

flat-leaf parsley, to garnish

SPICY MANGO RELISH:
1 ripe mango

2 tbsp cider vinegar
2 tbsp light muscovado sugar
1/2 tsp ground cinnamon
1/2 tsp ground ginger

1 To make the spicy mango relish, cut the mango lengthwise down both sides of the large, flat stone and discard the stone. Peel the mango and cut the flesh into evenly-sized chunks.

2 Place the cider vinegar, sugar, cinnamon and ginger in a small pan and heat gently, stirring continuously, until the sugar dissolves.

3 Stir the mango into the mixture in the pan and cook gently at the side of the barbecue (grill) or on

the stove for about 5 minutes or until the mango is soft.

4 Barbecue (grill) the chops on an oiled rack for about 4 minutes on each side.

5 Combine the mango chutney (relish) and chilli sauce in a small bowl and brush the glaze over the chops.

6 Continue to barbecue (grill) for a few more minutes on each side until the lamb is cooked, turning and basting frequently with

the mango chutney (relish) and chilli glaze.

7 Garnish and serve with grilled vegetables and the spicy mango relish.

VARIATION

The relish can also be served cold. Simmer the combined ingredients for 5 minutes, then remove from the heat and allow to cool. Leave to chill in the refrigerator until required. You can also use the mango chutney (relish) and chilli glaze on other cuts of lamb or on pork chops.

Indian Kofta

Makes 8

INGREDIENTS

1 small onion
450 g/1 lb minced lamb
2 tbsp curry paste
2 tbsp natural yogurt
oil, to baste
sprigs of fresh coriander
    (cilantro), to garnish

TOMATO SAMBAL:
3 tomatoes, deseeded and
    diced
pinch of ground coriander
pinch of ground cumin
2 tsp chopped, fresh coriander
    (cilantro)

salt and pepper

TO SERVE:
poppadoms
chutney (relish)

1 Put the onion in a food processor and chop finely. Add the lamb and process briefly to chop the mince further. Chopping the mince again will help the meat mixture to hold together during cooking. If you do not have a food processor, grate the onion finely before mixing it with the lamb.

2 Add the curry paste and yogurt and mix well. Divide the mixture into 8 equal portions.

3 Press and shape the mixture into 8 sausage shapes and push each one on to a skewer, pressing the mixture together firmly so that it holds its shape. Leave to chill in the refrigerator for at least 30 minutes or until required.

4 To make the tomato sambal, mix together the tomatoes, spices, chopped coriander (cilantro) and salt and pepper to taste in a bowl. Leave to stand for at least

30 minutes for the flavours to combine.

5 Barbecue (grill) the kebabs (kabobs) on an oiled rack over hot coals for 10–15 minutes, turning frequently. Baste with a little oil if required.

6 Transfer to serving plates and garnish with fresh coriander (cilantro). Serve accompanied with poppadoms, chutney (relish) and the tomato sambal.

Sweet Lamb Fillet

Serves 4

INGREDIENTS

2 fillets of neck of lamb, each
   225 g/8 oz
1 tbsp olive oil
1/2 onion, chopped finely
1 clove garlic, crushed
2.5 cm/1 inch piece root
   (fresh) ginger, grated

5 tbsp apple juice
3 tbsp smooth apple sauce
1 tbsp light muscovado sugar
1 tbsp tomato ketchup
   (catsup)
1/2 tsp mild mustard
salt and pepper

green salad leaves, croûtons
   and fresh crusty bread, to
   serve

1 Place the lamb fillet on a large piece of double thickness kitchen foil. Season with salt and pepper to taste.

2 Heat the oil in a small pan and fry the onion and garlic for 2–3 minutes until softened but not browned. Stir in the grated ginger and cook for 1 minute, stirring occasionally.

3 Stir in the apple juice, apple sauce, sugar, ketchup (catsup) and mustard and bring to the boil. Boil rapidly for about 10 minutes until reduced by half. Stir the mixture occasionally so that it does not burn and stick to the base of the pan.

4 Brush half of the sauce over the lamb, then wrap up the lamb in the kitchen foil to completely enclose it. Barbecue (grill) over hot coals for about 25 minutes, turning the parcel over occasionally.

5 Open out the kitchen foil and brush the lamb with some of the sauce. Continue to barbecue (grill) for a further 15–20 minutes or until cooked through.

6 Place the lamb on a chopping board, remove the foil and cut into thick slices. Transfer to serving plates and spoon over the remaining sauce. Serve with green salad leaves, croûtons and fresh crusty bread.

Lamb Noisettes with Tomato Salsa

Serves 4

INGREDIENTS

8 lamb noisettes
4 basil leaves
2 tbsp olive oil
grated rind and juice of
  $^1/_2$ lime
salt and pepper

sprig of fresh basil, to garnish
green salads leaves, to serve

SALSA:
6 tomatoes
4 basil leaves

8 stuffed green olives
1 tbsp lime juice
pinch of caster (superfine)
  sugar

1 Place the lamb noisettes in a shallow, non-metallic dish. Tear the basil leaves into pieces and scatter them over the lamb.

2 Drizzle the oil and lime juice over the lamb and add the lime rind. Season with salt and pepper to taste. Cover and leave to marinate in the refrigerator for at least 1 hour or preferably overnight.

3 To make the salsa, skin the tomatoes by cutting a small cross at the stem. Drop the tomatoes into boiling water for about 30 seconds, remove with a perforated spoon and then peel off the skins.

4 Cut the tomatoes in half, then scoop out the seeds and discard them. Cut the tomato flesh into large dice. Tear the basil leaves into pieces. Chop the olives. Mix together the tomatoes, basil, olives, lime juice and sugar in a bowl and leave for at least 1 hour or until required.

5 Remove the lamb from the marinade, reserving the marinade for basting. Barbecue (grill) over hot coals for 10–15 minutes, turning once and basting with the marinade.

6 Garnish with a sprig of basil and serve with the tomato salsa and green salad leaves.

Caribbean Pork

Serves 4

INGREDIENTS

4 pork loin chops

4 tbsp dark muscovado sugar

4 tbsp orange or pineapple juice

2 tbsp Jamaican rum

1 tbsp desiccated (shredded) coconut

1/2 tsp ground cinnamon

mixed salad leaves, to serve

COCONUT RICE:

225 g/8 oz/1 cup Basmati rice

450 ml/16 fl oz/2 cups water

150 ml/5 fl oz/²/3 cup coconut milk

4 tbsp raisins

4 tbsp roasted peanuts or cashew nuts

salt and pepper

2 tbsp desiccated (shredded) coconut, toasted

1 Trim any excess fat from the pork and place the chops in a shallow, non-metallic dish.

2 Combine the sugar, fruit juice, rum, coconut and cinnamon in a bowl, stirring until the sugar dissolves. Pour the mixture over the pork and leave to marinate in the refrigerator for at least 2 hours.

3 Remove the pork from the marinade,

reserving the liquid for basting. Barbecue (grill) over hot coals for 15–20 minutes, basting with the marinade.

4 Meanwhile, make the coconut rice. Rinse the rice under cold water, place it in a pan with the water and coconut milk and bring gently to the boil. Stir, cover and reduce the heat. Simmer gently for 12 minutes or until the rice is tender and the liquid has

been absorbed. Fluff up with a fork.

5 Stir the raisins and nuts into the rice, season with salt and pepper to taste and sprinkle with the coconut. Transfer the pork and rice to warm serving plates and serve with the mixed salad leaves.

Ham Steaks with Spicy Apple Rings

Serves 4

INGREDIENTS

4 ham steaks, each about 175 g/6 oz
1–2 tsp wholegrain mustard
1 tbsp honey
2 tbsp lemon juice

1 tbsp sunflower oil

APPLE RINGS:
2 green dessert (eating) apples
2 tsp demerara sugar

1/4 tsp ground nutmeg
1/4 tsp ground cinnamon
1/4 tsp ground allspice
1–2 tbsp melted butter

1 Using a pair of scissors, make a few cuts around the edges of the ham steaks to prevent them from curling up as they cook. Spread a little wholegrain mustard over the steaks.

2 Mix together the honey, lemon juice and oil in a bowl.

3 To prepare the apple rings, core the apples and cut them into thick slices. Mix the sugar with the spices and press the apple slices in the mixture until they are well coated on both sides.

4 Barbecue (grill) the steaks over hot coals for 3–4 minutes on each side, frequently basting with the honey and lemon mixture to prevent the meat from drying out during cooking.

5 Brush the apple slices with a little melted butter and barbecue (grill) alongside the pork for 3–4 minutes, turning once and brushing with melted butter as they cook.

6 Serve with the apple slices as a garnish.

COOK'S TIP

If you have time, soak the steaks in cold water for 30–60 minutes before cooking – this process will remove the excess salt.

Pork & Apple Skewers with Mustard

Makes 4

INGREDIENTS

450 g/1 lb pork fillet
2 (dessert) eating apples
a little lemon juice
1 lemon

2 tsp wholegrain mustard
2 tsp Dijon mustard
2 tbsp apple or orange juice
2 tbsp sunflower oil
crusty brown bread, to serve

MUSTARD SAUCE:
1 tbsp wholegrain mustard
1 tsp Dijon mustard
6 tbsp single (light) cream

1 To make the mustard sauce, combine the mustards in a small bowl and slowly blend in the cream. Leave to stand while you prepare the pork and apple skewers.

2 Cut the pork fillet into bite-size pieces and set aside until required.

3 Core the apples, then cut them into thick wedges. Toss the apple wedges in a little lemon juice – this will prevent any discoloration. Cut the lemon into slices.

4 Thread the pork, apple and lemon slices alternately on to 4 skewers.

5 Mix together the mustards, fruit juice and oil. Brush the mixture over the kebabs (kabobs) and barbecue (grill) over hot coals for 10–15 minutes, turning and basting with the marinade.

6 Transfer the kebabs (kabobs) to warm serving plates and spoon over a little of the mustard sauce. Serve with fresh, crusty brown bread.

COOK'S TIP

There are many varieties of mustard available, including English, which is very hot, Dijon, which is milder, and wholegrain, which contains whole mustard seeds. Mustards flavoured with other ingredients, such as honey or chilli, are also available.

Pork Ribs with Plum Sauce

Serves 4-6

INGREDIENTS

900 g/2 lb pork spare ribs
2 tbsp sunflower oil
1 tsp sesame oil
2 cloves garlic, crushed

2.5 cm/1 inch piece root
(fresh) ginger, grated
150 ml/5 fl oz/²/₃ cup plum
sauce
2 tbsp dry sherry

2 tbsp Hoisin sauce
2 tbsp soy sauce
4-6 spring onions (scallions),
to garnish (optional)

1 To prepare the garnish, trim the spring onions (scallions) to about 7.5 cm/ 3 inches long. Slice both ends into strips, leaving the onion intact in the centre.

2 Put the spring onions (scallions) into a bowl of iced water for at least 30 minutes until the ends start to curl up. Leave them in the water and set aside until required.

3 If you buy the spare ribs in a single piece, cut them into individual ribs. Bring a large pan of water to the boil and add the ribs. Cook for 5 minutes, then drain thoroughly.

4 Heat the oils together in a pan, add the garlic and ginger and cook gently for 1–2 minutes to bring out the flavour. Stir in the plum sauce, sherry, Hoisin sauce and soy sauce and heat through.

5 Brush the sauce over the pork ribs. Barbecue (grill) over hot coals for 5–10 minutes, then move the ribs to a cooler part of the barbecue (grill). Barbecue (grill) for a further 15–20 minutes, basting with the remaining sauce. Garnish with the spring onion (scallion) brushes, and serve hot.

COOK'S TIP

Par-cooking the ribs in boiling water removes excess fat, which helps prevent the ribs from splitting during cooking. Do not be put off by the large quantity – there is only a little meat on each, but they are quite cheap.

Fruity Pork Skewers

Makes 4

INGREDIENTS

4 boneless pork loin steaks	slices of orange and lemon, to	2 tbsp olive oil
8 ready-to-eat prunes	garnish	1 tsp ground bay leaves
8 ready-to-eat dried apricots		salt and pepper
	MARINADE:	
	4 tbsp orange juice	

1 Trim the visible fat from the pork and cut the meat into evenly-sized chunks.

2 Place the pork in a shallow, non-metallic dish and add the prunes and apricots.

3 To make the marinade, mix together the orange juice, oil, bay leaves and salt and pepper to taste in a bowl.

4 Pour the marinade over the pork and fruit and toss until well coated.

Marinate in the refrigerator for at least 1 hour or preferably overnight.

5 Soak 4 wooden skewers in cold water to prevent them from catching alight on the barbecue (grill).

6 Remove the pork and fruit from the marinade, using a perforated spoon, reserving the marinade for basting. Thread the pork and fruit on to the skewers.

7 Barbecue (grill) the skewers on an oiled

rack over medium hot coals for 10–15 minutes, turning and frequently basting with the reserved marinade, or until the pork is cooked through.

8 Transfer the pork and fruit skewers to warm serving plates. Garnish with slices of orange and lemon and serve hot.

Spicy Pork Ribs

Serves 4-6

INGREDIENTS

900 g/2 lb pork spare ribs
150 ml/5 fl oz/²/₃ cup passata
(sieved tomatoes)
2 tbsp red wine vinegar

2 tbsp dark muscovado sugar
1 clove garlic, crushed
1 tsp dried thyme
¹/₂ tsp dried rosemary

1 tsp chilli sauce
red chillies, to garnish
(optional)
mixed salad leaves, to serve

1 If you buy the spare ribs in a single piece, carefully cut them into individual ribs using a very sharp knife.

2 Bring a large pan of water to the boil and add the ribs. Cook the ribs for 10 minutes, then drain them thoroughly. Place the ribs in a large, shallow, non-metallic dish.

3 To make the spicy sauce, combine the passata (sieved tomatoes), red wine vinegar, sugar, garlic, dried thyme, dried rosemary and chilli

sauce in a bowl until well blended.

4 Pour the sauce over the pork ribs and toss to coat on all sides. Leave to marinate for 1 hour.

5 Remove the ribs from the sauce, reserving the sauce for basting. Barbecue (grill) the ribs over hot coals for 5–10 minutes, then move them to a cooler part of the barbecue (grill). Cook the ribs for a further 15–20 minutes, turning and basting frequently with the remaining sauce.

6 Transfer the ribs to warm serving plates and garnish with the red chillies (if using). Serve with the mixed salad leaves, if wished.

COOK'S TIP

For authentic American-style ribs make sure you buy pork spare ribs and not spare rib chops. Pork spare ribs are often sold cut into individual ribs, but it is quite easy to cut between the ribs with a sharp knife if you cannot buy them already separated.

Ham & Pineapple Kebabs (Kabobs)

Makes 4

INGREDIENTS

450 g/1 lb thick ham steak
425 g/15 oz can pineapple
    pieces, in natural juice
2 tbsp sunflower oil

225 g/8 oz firm Brie, chilled, or
    Emmenthal or Jarlsburg
1 clove garlic, crushed
1 tbsp lemon juice

$^1/_2$ tsp ground nutmeg
$^1/_4$ tsp ground cloves
pepper
cooked rice, to serve

1 Cut the ham into evenly-sized chunks.

2 Place the ham in a pan of boiling water and simmer for 5 minutes.

3 Drain the pineapple pieces and reserve 3 tbsp of the juice. Cut the cheese into large chunks.

4 To make the baste, combine the pineapple juice, oil, garlic, lemon juice, nutmeg, cloves and pepper to taste in a small screw-top jar and shake until well combined. Set aside until required.

5 Remove the ham from the pan with a perforated spoon. Thread the ham on to skewers, alternating with the pineapple and cheese pieces.

6 Barbecue (grill) the kebabs (kabobs) over warm coals, turning and basting frequently with the oil and pineapple juice mixture, for 2–4 minutes on each side. Barbecue (grill) the kebabs (kabobs) until the pineapple and ham are hot and the cheese is just beginning to melt. Serve the kebabs (kabobs) on a bed of cooked rice.

COOK'S TIP

Cook the skewers on the barbecue (grill) just long enough to reheat the gammon and to warm the pineapple. Take care not to overcook the kebabs (kabobs) or you will end up with a gooey mess – the cheese should only just begin to melt.

Honey-glazed Pork Chops

Serves 4

INGREDIENTS

4 lean pork loin chops	4 tbsp orange juice	salt and pepper
4 tbsp clear honey	2 tbsp olive oil	
1 tbsp dry sherry	2.5 cm/1 inch piece root (fresh) ginger, grated	

1 Season the pork chops with salt and pepper to taste. Set aside while you make the glaze.

2 To make the glaze, place the honey, sherry, orange juice, oil and ginger in a small pan and heat gently, stirring continuously, until all of the ingredients are well blended.

3 Barbecue (grill) the chops on an oiled rack over hot coals for about 5 minutes on each side.

4 Brush the chops with the glaze and barbecue (grill) for a further 2–4 minutes on each side, basting frequently with the glaze.

5 Transfer the chops to warm serving plates and serve hot.

COOK'S TIP

To give the recipe a little more punch, stir $1/2$ teaspoon of chilli sauce or 1 tablespoon of wholegrain mustard into the basting glaze.

VARIATION

This recipe works equally well with lamb chops and with chicken portions, such as thighs or drumsticks. Barbecue (grill) the meat in exactly the same way as in this recipe, basting frequently with the honey glaze – the result will be just as delicious!

Sausages with Barbecue Sauce

Serves 4

INGREDIENTS

2 tbsp sunflower oil
1 large onion, chopped
2 cloves garlic, chopped
225 g/8 oz can chopped
    tomatoes
1 tbsp Worcestershire sauce

2 tbsp brown fruity sauce
2 tbsp light muscovado sugar
4 tbsp white wine vinegar
$1/2$ tsp mild chilli powder
$1/4$ tsp mustard powder

dash of Tabasco sauce
450 g/1 lb sausages
salt and pepper
bread finger rolls, to serve

1 To make the sauce, heat the oil in a small pan and fry the onion and garlic for 4–5 minutes until softened and just beginning to brown.

2 Add the tomatoes, Worcestershire sauce, brown fruity sauce, sugar, wine vinegar, chilli powder, mustard powder, Tabasco sauce and salt and pepper to taste to the pan and bring to the boil.

3 Reduce the heat and simmer gently for

10–15 minutes until the sauce begins to thicken slightly. Stir occasionally so that the sauce does not burn and stick to the bottom of the pan. Set aside and keep warm until required.

4 Barbecue (grill) the sausages over hot coals for 10–15 minutes, turning them frequently. Do not prick the sausages with a fork or the juices and fat will run out and cause the barbecue (grill) to flare up.

5 Insert the sausages into the bread rolls and serve with the barbecue sauce.

COOK'S TIP

Lincolnshire sausages are a good choice as are Cumberland sausages (secure the coil with skewers so that it does not unravel as it cooks). Venison sausages have a good, gamey flavour. Black pudding can be used if cut into thick slices, as can strong continental sausages.

Tangy Pork Fillet

Serves 4

INGREDIENTS

400 g/14 oz pork fillet
3 tbsp orange marmalade
grated rind and juice of
  1 orange
1 tbsp white wine vinegar
dash of Tabasco sauce
salt and pepper

SAUCE:
1 tbsp olive oil
1 small onion, chopped
1 small green (bell) pepper,
  deseeded and thinly sliced
1 tbsp cornflour (cornstarch)

150 ml/5 fl oz/²⁄₃ cup orange
  juice

TO SERVE:
cooked rice
mixed salad leaves

1 Place a large piece of double thickness foil in a shallow dish. Put the pork fillet in the centre of the foil and season.

2 Heat the marmalade, orange rind and juice, vinegar and Tabasco sauce in a small pan, stirring until the marmalade melts and the ingredients combine.

3 Pour the mixture over the pork and wrap the meat in foil, making sure that the parcel is well sealed so that the juices cannot run out. Place over hot coals and barbecue (grill) for about 25 minutes, turning occasionally.

4 Heat the oil and cook the onion for 2–3 minutes until softened. Add the (bell) pepper and cook for 3–4 minutes.

5 Remove the pork from the kitchen foil and place on to the rack. Pour the cooking juices into the pan containing the sauce.

6 Barbecue (grill) the pork for a further 10–20 minutes, turning, until cooked through and golden on the outside.

7 Mix the cornflour with a little orange juice to form a paste. Add to the sauce with the remaining cooking juices. Cook, stirring, until the sauce thickens.

8 Cut the pork into slices. Spoon over the sauce and serve.

Pork & Sage Kebabs (Kabobs)

Makes 12

INGREDIENTS

450 g/1 lb pork mince
25 g/1 oz fresh breadcrumbs
1 small onion, chopped very
  finely
1 tbsp fresh sage, chopped
2 tbsp apple sauce

¹/4 tsp ground nutmeg
salt and pepper

BASTE:
3 tbsp olive oil
1 tbsp lemon juice

TO SERVE:
6 small pitta breads
mixed salad leaves
6 tbsp thick, natural yogurt

1 Place the mince in a mixing bowl together with the breadcrumbs, onion, sage, apple sauce, nutmeg and salt and pepper to taste. Mix until the ingredients are well combined.

2 Using your hands, shape the mixture into small balls, about the size of large marbles, and leave to chill in the refrigerator for at least 30 minutes.

3 Meanwhile, soak 12 small wooden skewers in cold water for at least 30 minutes. Thread the meatballs on to them.

4 To make the baste, mix together the oil and lemon juice in a small bowl, whisking with a fork until it is well blended.

5 Barbecue (grill) the kebabs (kabobs) over hot coals for 8–10 minutes, turning and basting frequently with the lemon and oil mixture, until golden and cooked through.

6 Line the pitta breads with the salad leaves and spoon over some of the yogurt. Serve with the kebabs (kabobs).

VARIATION

Save time by shaping the meat mixture into burgers. Leave to chill for at least 20 minutes, then barbecue (grill), basting with the oil and lemon mixture for 15 minutes, turning once. Serve in burger buns topped with a little apple sauce.

Steak & Kidney Kebabs (Kabobs)

Makes 4

INGREDIENTS

350 g/12 oz rump steak
2 lamb's kidneys
1 small onion, sliced
$^{1}/_{2}$ tsp dried rosemary

150 ml/5 fl oz/$^{2}/_{3}$ cup brown
ale (beer)
8 button mushrooms
8 bay leaves
4 tbsp sunflower oil

TO SERVE:
cooked rice
cherry tomatoes

1 Using a sharp knife, trim the steak and cut it into evenly-sized pieces.

2 Cut the kidneys in half and remove the skin. Snip out the core and cut each kidney half into half again.

3 Place the steak and kidney pieces in a shallow, non-metallic dish.

4 Add the onions and rosemary to the dish and pour over the beer. Cover and leave to marinate in the refrigerator for at least 4 hours or preferably overnight.

5 Remove the meat from the marinade, reserving 4 tbsp of the marinade for basting.

6 Thread the steak and kidney pieces on to the skewers, alternating with the mushrooms and the bay leaves.

7 Stir the oil into the reserved marinade. Barbecue (grill) the kebabs (kabobs) over hot coals for 8–10 minutes, turning and basting with the reserved marinade. Take care not to overcook the kidneys.

8 Serve on a bed of cooked rice and with a few cherry tomatoes.

COOK'S TIP

To save time, prepare and marinate the kebabs (kabobs) a day in advance. Marinade them in a shallow dish, and turn occasionally to make sure they are completely coated.

Mixed Grill Skewers

Serves 4

INGREDIENTS

225 g/8 oz lamb neck fillet
4 lamb's kidneys
4 thick sausages
8 rashers rindless, streaky
   bacon

BASTE:
4 tbsp olive oil
2 tbsp lemon juice
1 tbsp fresh mixed herbs,
   chopped

TO SERVE:
2 beef steak tomatoes
4 flat mushrooms

1 Cut the lamb fillet into evenly-sized pieces. Skin and core the kidneys and cut each into 4 pieces.

2 Twist the sausages in the centre and cut each sausage in half.

3 Stretch out the bacon rashers with the back of a knife.

4 Either wrap the bacon around the sausages or simply roll up the rashers on their own. Thread the lamb, sausage, bacon and kidneys on to skewers.

5 To make the baste, mix together the oil, lemon juice and mixed herbs and leave to stand until required.

6 Barbecue (grill) the kebabs (kabobs) over hot coals, turning and basting frequently, for 8–10 minutes.

7 Cut the tomatoes and mushrooms into large chunks and thread them on to separate skewers. Barbecue (grill) the tomato and mushroom skewers next to the meat for

5 minutes, turning and basting frequently.

8 Transfer the meat skewers to serving plates and serve hot with the tomato and mushroom skewers.

COOK'S TIP

All the elements of this dish can be cooked directly on the barbecue (grill). However, threading them on to skewers makes them quicker and less fiddly to turn and baste.

Liver & Onion Kebabs (Kabobs)

Makes 4

INGREDIENTS

350 g/12 oz lamb's liver
2 tbsp seasoned plain (all-
purpose) flour
$^{1}/_{2}$ tsp dried mixed herbs

125 g/4$^{1}/_{2}$ oz rindless streaky
bacon
2 medium onions
75 g/2$^{3}/_{4}$ oz butter

2 tsp balsamic vinegar

TO SERVE:
mixed salad leaves
tomato quarters

1 Cut the lamb's liver into bite-sized pieces. Then mix the flour with the dried mixed herbs and toss the liver in the seasoned flour.

2 Stretch out the bacon rashers with the back of a knife. Cut each rasher in half and wrap the bacon around half of the liver pieces.

3 Thread the plain liver pieces on to skewers, alternating them with the bacon-wrapped liver pieces.

4 Cut the onions into rings and thread over the kebabs (kabobs). Finely chop the onion rings that are too small to thread over the kebabs (kabobs).

5 Heat the butter in a small pan and sauté the chopped onions for about 5 minutes until softened. Stir in the vinegar.

6 Brush the butter mixture over the kebabs (kabobs) and barbecue (grill) over hot coals for 8–10 minutes, basting occasionally with

the butter mixture, until the liver is just cooked but is still a little pink inside.

7 Transfer the kebabs (kabobs) to serving plates. Serve with mixed salad leaves and tomatoes.

COOK'S TIP

Choose thick slices of liver to give good-sized pieces. Use bacon to hold 2–3 pieces of thinner liver together if necessary.

Vegetables & Salads

Vegetarians need never feel left out as many vegetables cook well on the barbecue (grill), and they taste delicious. Try the Colourful Vegetable Kebabs (Kabobs), the Nutty Rice Burgers, the Vegetarian Sausages or the delicious Marinated Tofu (Bean Curd) Kebabs (Kabobs). Cook vegetables whole, sliced on skewers or in parcels for main dishes or as tasty side dishes.

Keep your diners happy while they wait for the main course with some tasty nibbles, such as Crispy Potato Skins, Garlic Bread or Mediterranean Bruschetta, while Stuffed Mushrooms and Stuffed Tomatoes make ideal starters for your vegetarian guests.

If you need inspiration for salads to accompany your barbecued (grilled) food, look no further. All the salads in this chapter go well with barbecued (grilled) dishes, and many make ideal starters. Pear & Roquefort Salad and Artichoke & Parma Ham (Prosciutto) salad are stylish starters that can be prepared well in advance.

Marinated Tofu (Bean Curd) Skewers

Serves 4

INGREDIENTS

350 g/12 oz tofu (bean curd)	slices of lemon, to garnish	1 clove garlic, crushed
1 red (bell) pepper		$1/2$ tsp fresh rosemary,
1 yellow (bell) pepper	MARINADE:	chopped
2 courgettes (zucchini)	grated rind and juice of	$1/2$ tsp chopped, fresh thyme
8 button mushrooms	$1/2$ lemon	1 tbsp walnut oil

1 To make the marinade, combine the lemon rind and juice, garlic, rosemary, thyme and oil in a shallow dish.

2 Drain the tofu (bean curd), pat it dry on kitchen paper and cut it into squares. Add to the marinade and toss to coat. Leave to marinate for 20–30 minutes.

3 Meanwhile, deseed and cut the (bell) peppers into 2.5 cm/1 inch pieces. Blanch in boiling water for 4 minutes,

refresh in cold water and drain well.

4 Using a canelle knife (or potato peeler), remove strips of peel from the courgettes (zucchini). Cut the courgette (zucchini) into 2.5 cm/1 inch chunks.

5 Remove the tofu (bean curd) from the marinade, reserving the liquid for basting. Thread the tofu (bean curd) on to 8 skewers, alternating with the (bell) peppers, courgette (zucchini) and button mushrooms.

6 Barbecue (grill) the skewers over medium hot coals for about 6 minutes, turning and basting with the marinade.

7 Transfer the skewers to warm serving plates, garnish with slices of lemon and serve.

VARIATION

For a spicy kebab (kabob), make a marinade from 1 tablespoon of curry paste, 2 tablespoons of oil and the juice of $1/2$ lemon.

Crispy Potato Skins

Serves 4-6

INGREDIENTS

8 small baking potatoes, scrubbed
50 g/1¾ oz butter, melted
salt and pepper

OPTIONAL TOPPING:
6 spring onions (scallions), sliced

50 g/1¾ oz salami, cut into thin strips
50 g/1¾ oz grated gruyère cheese

1 Preheat the oven to 200°C/400°F/Gas Mark 6. Prick the potatoes with a fork and bake for 1 hour or until tender. Alternatively, cook in a microwave on High for 12–15 minutes.

2 Cut the potatoes in half and scoop out the flesh, leaving about 5 mm/¼ inch potato flesh lining the skin.

3 Brush inside the potato with melted butter.

4 Place the skins, cut-side down, over medium hot coals and barbecue (grill) for 10–15 minutes. Turn the potato skins over and barbecue (grill) for a further 5 minutes or until they are crispy. Take care that they do not burn.

5 Season the potato skins with salt and pepper to taste and serve while they are still warm.

6 If wished, the skins can filled with a variety of toppings. Barbecue (grill) the potato skins as above for about 10 minutes, then turn cut-side up and sprinkle with slices of spring onion (scallion), grated cheese and chopped salami. Barbecue (grill) for a further 5 minutes until the cheese begins to melt. Serve hot.

COOK'S TIP

Potato skins can be served on their own but they are delicious served with a dip. Try a spicy tomato or hummus dip.

Spicy Sweet Potato Slices

Serves 4

INGREDIENTS

450 g/1 lb sweet potatoes	1 tsp chilli sauce
2 tbsp sunflower oil	salt and pepper

1 Bring a large pan of water to the boil, add the sweet potatoes and par-boil them for 10 minutes. Drain thoroughly and transfer to a chopping board.

2 Peel the potatoes and cut them into thick slices.

3 Mix together the oil, chilli sauce and salt and pepper to taste in a small bowl.

4 Brush the spicy mixture liberally over one side of the potatoes. Place the potatoes, oil side down, over medium hot coals and barbecue (grill) for 5–6 minutes.

5 Lightly brush the tops of the potatoes with the oil, turn them over and barbecue (grill) for a further 5 minutes or until crisp and golden. Transfer the potatoes to a warm serving dish and serve.

COOK'S TIP

Although it is a vegetable the sweet potato is used in both sweet and savoury dishes. It is very versatile and can be boiled, roasted, fried, or cooked as here over a barbecue (grill).

VARIATION

For a simple spicy dip combine 150 ml/5 fl oz/ ²⁄₃ cup sour cream with ½ teaspoon of sugar, ½ teaspoon of Dijon mustard and salt and pepper to taste. Leave to chill until required.

Barbecued Garlic Potato Wedges

Serves 4

INGREDIENTS

3 large baking potatoes, scrubbed	2 garlic cloves, chopped	1 tbsp chopped, fresh thyme
4 tbsp olive oil	1 tbsp chopped, fresh rosemary	salt and pepper
25 g/1 oz butter	1 tbsp chopped, fresh parsley	

1 Bring a large pan of water to the boil, add the potatoes and par-boil them for 10 minutes. Drain the potatoes, refresh under cold water and drain them again thoroughly.

2 Transfer the potatoes to a chopping board. When the potatoes are cold enough to handle, cut them into thick wedges, but do not remove the skins.

3 Heat the oil and butter in a small pan together with the garlic. Cook gently until the garlic begins to brown, then remove the pan from the heat.

4 Stir the herbs and salt and pepper to taste into the mixture in the pan.

5 Brush the herb mixture over the potatoes.

6 Barbecue (grill) the potatoes over hot coals for 10–15 minutes, brushing liberally with any of the remaining herb and butter mixture, or until the potatoes are just tender.

7 Transfer the barbecued garlic potatoes to a warm serving plate and serve as a starter or as a side dish.

COOK'S TIP

You may find it easier to barbecue (grill) these potatoes in a hinged rack or in a specially designed barbecue (grill) roasting tray.

Vegetarian Sausages

Makes 8

INGREDIENTS

1 tbsp sunflower oil
1 small onion, chopped finely
50 g/1³/4 oz mushrooms,
    chopped finely
¹/2 red (bell) pepper, deseeded
    and chopped finely

400 g/14 oz can cannellini
    beans, rinsed and drained
100 g/3¹/2 oz fresh
    breadcrumbs
100 g/3¹/2 oz Cheddar cheese,
    grated
1 tsp dried mixed herbs

1 egg yolk
seasoned plain (all-purpose)
    flour
oil, to baste
bread rolls, slices of fried
    onion and tomato relish,
    to serve

1 Heat the oil in a saucepan and fry the prepared onion, mushrooms and (bell) peppers until softened.

2 Mash the cannellini beans in a large mixing bowl. Add the onion, mushroom and (bell) pepper mixture, the breadcrumbs, cheese, herbs and egg yolk, and mix together well.

3 Press the mixture together with your fingers and shape into 8 sausages.

4 Roll each sausage in the seasoned flour. Chill for 30 minutes.

5 Barbecue (grill) the sausages on a sheet of oiled foil set over medium coals for 15–20 minutes, turning and basting frequently with oil, until golden.

6 Split a bread roll down the middle and insert a layer of fried onions. Place the sausage in the roll and serve with tomato relish.

COOK'S TIP

Take care not to break the sausages when you turn them over. If you have a hinged rack, oil this and place the sausages inside, turning and oiling frequently.

Nutty Rice Burgers

Makes 6

INGREDIENTS

1 tbsp sunflower oil
1 small onion, chopped finely
100 g/3^1/2 oz mushrooms,
    chopped finely
350 g/12 oz/8 cups cooked
    brown rice
100 g/3^1/2 oz breadcrumbs
75 g/2^3/4 oz walnuts, chopped

1 egg
2 tbsp brown fruity sauce
dash of Tabasco sauce
salt and pepper
oil, to baste
6 individual cheese slices
    (optional)

TO SERVE:
6 sesame seed baps
slices of onion
slices of tomato
green salad leaves

1 Heat the oil in a pan and fry the onions for 3–4 minutes until they just begin to soften. Add the mushrooms and cook for a further 2 minutes.

2 Remove the pan from the heat and mix the rice, breadcrumbs, walnuts, egg and sauces into the vegetables. Season with salt and pepper and mix well.

3 Shape the mixture into 6 burgers, pressing the mixture together with your fingers. Leave to chill in the refrigerator for at least 30 minutes.

4 Barbecue (grill) the burgers on an oiled rack over medium coals for 5–6 minutes on each side, turning once and frequently basting with oil.

5 If liked, top the burgers with a slice of cheese 2 minutes before the end of the cooking time. Barbecue (grill) the onion and tomato slices.

6 Toast the sesame seed baps at the side of the barbecue. Serve the burgers in the baps, together with the barbecued (grilled) onions and tomatoes.

Aubergine (Eggplant) & Mozzarella Sandwiches

Serves 2

INGREDIENTS

1 large aubergine (eggplant)
1 tbsp lemon juice
3 tbsp olive oil
125 g/4^1/$_2$ oz grated
   Mozzarella cheese

2 sun-dried tomatoes,
   chopped
salt and pepper

TO SERVE:
Italian bread
mixed salad leaves
slices of tomato

1 Slice the aubergine (eggplant) into thin rounds.

2 Combine the lemon juice and oil in a bowl and season the mixture with salt and pepper.

3 Brush the aubergine (eggplant) slices with the oil and lemon juice mixture and barbecue (grill) over medium hot coals for 2–3 minutes, without turning, until they are golden on the under side.

4 Turn half of the aubergine (eggplant) slices over and sprinkle with cheese and chopped sun-dried tomatoes.

5 Place the remaining aubergine (eggplant) slices on top of the cheese and tomatoes, turning them so that the cooked side is uppermost.

6 Barbecue (grill) for 1–2 minutes, then carefully turn the sandwich over and barbecue (grill)

for 1–2 minutes. Baste with the oil mixture.

7 Serve with Italian bread, mixed salad leaves and tomato.

VARIATION

Try Feta cheese instead of Mozzarella but omit the salt from the basting oil. A creamy goat's cheese would be equally delicious.

Char-grilled Aubergine (Eggplant)

Serves 4

INGREDIENTS

1 large aubergine (eggplant)	PESTO:	CUCUMBER SAUCE:
3 tbsp olive oil	1 clove garlic	150 g/5$^{1}/_{2}$ oz natural yogurt
1 tsp sesame oil	25 g/1 oz pine nuts	5 cm/2 inch cucumber
salt and pepper	15 g/$^{1}/_{2}$ oz fresh basil leaves	$^{1}/_{2}$ tsp mint sauce
	2 tbsp Parmesan cheese	
	6 tbsp olive oil	
	salt and pepper	

1 Remove the stalk from the aubergine (eggplant), then cut it lengthwise into 8 thin slices.

2 Lay the slices on a plate or board and sprinkle them liberally with salt to remove the bitter juices. Leave to stand.

3 Meanwhile, prepare the baste. Combine the olive and sesame oils, season with pepper and set aside.

4 To make the pesto, put the garlic, pine nuts, basil and cheese in a food processor until finely chopped. With the machine running, gradually add the oil in a thin stream. Season to taste.

5 To make the minty cucumber sauce, place the yogurt in a mixing bowl. Remove the seeds from the cucumber and dice the flesh finely. Stir into the yogurt with the mint sauce.

6 Rinse the aubergine (eggplant) slices and pat them dry on absorbent kitchen paper. Baste with the oil mixture and barbecue (grill) over hot coals for about 10 minutes, turning once. The aubergine (eggplant) should be golden and tender.

7 Transfer the aubergine (eggplant) slices to serving plates and serve with either the cucumber sauce or the pesto.

Stuffed Tomatoes

Makes 8

INGREDIENTS

4 beefsteak tomatoes
300 g/10^1/2 oz/4^1/2 cups
    cooked rice
8 spring onions (scallions),
    chopped

3 tbsp chopped, fresh mint
2 tbsp chopped, fresh parsley
3 tbsp pine nuts
3 tbsp raisins
2 tsp olive oil

salt and pepper

1 Cut the tomatoes in half, then scoop out the seeds and discard.

2 Stand the tomatoes upside down on absorbent kitchen paper for a few moments in order for the juices to drain out.

3 Turn the tomatoes the right way up and sprinkle the insides with salt and pepper.

4 Mix together the rice, spring onions (scallions), mint, parsley, pine nuts and raisins.

Spoon the mixture into the tomato cups.

5 Drizzle over a little olive oil, then barbecue (grill) the tomatoes on an oiled rack over medium hot coals for about 10 minutes until they are tender.

6 Transfer the tomatoes to serving plates and serve immediately.

COOK'S TIP

Tomatoes are a popular barbecue (grill) vegetable and can be quickly cooked. Try grilling (broiling) slices of beefsteak tomato and slices of onion brushed with a little oil and topped with sprigs of fresh herbs. In addition, cherry tomatoes can be threaded on to skewers and barbecued (grilled) for 5–10 minutes until hot.

Colourful Vegetable Kebabs (Kabobs)

Serves 4

INGREDIENTS

1 red (bell) pepper, deseeded	1 small onion	SEASONED OIL:
1 yellow (bell) pepper, deseeded	8 cherry tomatoes	6 tbsp olive oil
	100 g/3¹/₂ oz wild mushrooms	1 clove garlic, crushed
1 green (bell) pepper, deseeded		¹/₂ tsp mixed dried herbs or herbes de Provence

1 Cut the (bell) peppers into 2.5 cm/1 inch pieces.

2 Peel the onion and cut it into wedges, leaving the root end just intact to help keep the wedges together.

3 Thread the (bell) peppers, onion wedges, tomatoes and mushrooms on to skewers, alternating the colours of the (bell) peppers.

4 To make the seasoned oil, mix together the oil, garlic and herbs in a small bowl. Brush the mixture liberally over the kebabs (kabobs).

5 Barbecue (grill) the kebabs (kabobs) over medium hot coals for 10–15 minutes, brushing with more of the seasoned oil and turning the skewers frequently.

6 Transfer the vegetable kebabs (kabobs) to warm serving plates. Serve the kebabs (kabobs) with walnut sauce (see Cook's Tip, right), if you wish.

COOK'S TIP

These kebabs (kabobs) are delicious when accompanied with a walnut sauce. To make the sauce, process 125 g/4 ¹/₂ oz walnuts in a food processor until they form a smooth paste. With the machine running, add 150 ml/5 fl oz/²/₃ cup double (heavy) cream and 1 tablespoon of olive oil. Season to taste. Alternatively, finely chop the walnuts then pound them in a pestle and mortar to form a paste. Mix with the cream and oil, and season.

Char-grilled Mixed Vegetables

Serves 4-6

INGREDIENTS
---

8 baby aubergines (eggplants)
4 courgettes (zucchini)
2 red onions
4 tomatoes

salt and pepper
1 tsp balsamic vinegar, to serve

BASTE:
75 g/2¾ oz butter
2 tsp walnut oil
2 cloves garlic, chopped
4 tbsp dry white wine or cider

---

1 Cut the aubergines (eggplants) in half. Trim and cut the courgettes (zucchini) in half lengthwise. Thickly slice the onions and halve the tomatoes.

2 Season all of the vegetables with salt and pepper to taste.

3 To make the baste, melt the butter with the oil in a saucepan. Add the garlic and cook gently for 1–2 minutes. Remove the pan from the heat and stir in the wine or cider.

4 Add the vegetables to the pan and toss them in the baste mixture. You may need to do this in several batches to ensure that all of the vegetables are coated evenly with the baste mixture.

5 Remove the vegetables from the baste mixture, reserving any excess baste. Place the vegetables on an oiled rack over medium hot coals. Barbecue (grill) them for 15–20 minutes, basting with the reserved baste mixture and turning once or twice during cooking.

6 Transfer the vegetables to warm serving plates and serve sprinkled with balsamic vinegar.

COOK'S TIP

Use a long-handled brush for basting food on the barbecue (grill).

Stuffed Mushrooms

Makes 12

INGREDIENTS

12 open-cap mushrooms
4 spring onions (scallions),
   chopped
4 tsp olive oil

100 g/3^1/$_2$ oz fresh brown
   breadcrumbs
1 tsp fresh oregano, chopped

100 g/3^1/$_2$ oz Feta cheese or
   chorizo sausage

1 Remove the stalks from the mushrooms and chop the stalks finely.

2 Sauté the mushroom stalks and spring onions (scallions) in half of the oil.

3 In a bowl, mix the mushroom stalks and spring onions (scallions). Add the breadcrumbs and oregano to the mushrooms and spring onions (scallions), mix and set aside.

4 If using Feta, crumble the cheese into small pieces in a small bowl.

5 If you are using chorizo sausage, remove the skin and chop the flesh finely.

6 Add the cheese or chorizo to the breadcrumb mixture and mix well.

7 Spoon the stuffing mixture into the mushroom caps. Drizzle the oil over the mushrooms. Barbecue (grill) on an oiled rack over medium hot coals for 8–10 minutes. Transfer the mushrooms to serving plates and serve hot.

COOK'S TIP

If using small mushrooms, place a sheet of oiled kitchen foil on top of the barbecue (grill) rack and cook the mushrooms on this. This will stop the mushrooms from cooking too quickly and burning, and will prevent any excess stuffing from dropping on the coals.

Corn-on-the-cob

Serves 4

INGREDIENTS

4 cobs of sweetcorn, with
husks
100 g/3$^{1}/_{2}$ oz butter

1 tbsp chopped, fresh parsley
1 tsp chopped, fresh chives
1 tsp chopped, fresh thyme

rind of 1 lemon, grated
salt and pepper

1 To prepare the cobs of sweetcorn, peel back the husks and remove the silken hairs.

2 Fold back the husks and secure them in place with string if necessary.

3 Blanch the cobs of sweetcorn in a large pan of boiling water for about 5 minutes. Remove the cobs with a perforated spoon and drain.

4 Barbecue (grill) the cobs over medium hot coals for 20–30 minutes, turning frequently.

5 Meanwhile, soften the butter and beat in the parsley, chives, thyme, lemon rind and salt and pepper to taste.

6 Transfer the cobs of sweetcorn to serving plates, remove the string and pull back the husks. Serve with a generous portion of herb butter.

COOK'S TIP

When you are buying fresh sweetcorn, look for plump, tightly packed kernels. If you are unable to get fresh cobs, cook frozen sweetcorn cobs on the barbecue (grill). Spread some of the herb butter on to a sheet of double thickness kitchen foil. Wrap the cobs in the foil and barbecue (grill) among the coals for 20–30 minutes.

Pumpkin Parcels with Chilli & Lime

Serves 4

INGREDIENTS

700 g/1 lb 9oz pumpkin or squash	25 g/1 oz butter	2 tsp lime juice
2 tbsp sunflower oil	1/2 tsp chilli sauce	
	rind of 1 lime, grated	

1 Halve the pumpkin or squash and scoop out the seeds. Rinse the seeds and reserve. Cut the pumpkin into thin wedges and peel.

2 Heat the oil and butter together in a large saucepan, stirring continuously until melted. Stir in the chilli sauce, lime rind and juice.

3 Add the pumpkin or squash and seeds to the pan and toss to coat in the flavoured butter.

4 Divide the mixture among 4 double thickness sheets of kitchen foil. Fold over the kitchen foil to enclose the pumpkin or squash mixture.

5 Barbecue (grill) the foil parcels for 15–25 minutes or until the pumpkin or squash is tender.

6 Transfer the foil parcels to warm serving plates. Open the parcels at the table and serve at once.

VARIATION

Add 2 teaspoons of curry paste to the oil instead of the lime and chilli.

COOK'S TIP

It is a good idea to wear disposable gloves when slicing and deseeding chillies. Alternatively, rub a little oil over your fingers before you begin – the oil will help to prevent your skin absorbing the chilli juice. Wash your hands thoroughly afterwards.

Garlic Bread

Serves 6

INGREDIENTS

150 g/5¹/2 oz butter, softened
3 cloves garlic, crushed

2 tbsp chopped, fresh parsley
pepper

1 large or 2 small sticks of
French bread

1 Mix together the butter, garlic and parsley in a bowl until well combined. Season to taste with a little pepper and mix well.

2 Cut the French bread into thick slices.

3 Spread the flavoured butter over one side of each slice and reassemble the loaf on a large sheet of thick kitchen foil.

4 Wrap the bread well and barbecue (grill) over hot coals for 10–15 minutes until the butter melts and the bread is piping hot.

5 Serve as an accompaniment to a wide range of dishes.

COOK'S TIP

Some recipes suggest that you do not cut all the way through the bread when you slice it, but you will find it a lot easier to serve if you do. Simply keep the slices in order and reassemble once buttered.

VARIATION

For a tasty variation, sprinkle a little grated Mozzarella cheese between each slice of bread. Reassemble the loaf and barbecue (grill) for 10–15 minutes, until the cheese has just melted.

COOK'S TIP

When garlic is cooked like this on a barbecue (grill), the sweetness of it comes to the fore. Garlic combines well with fresh, crusty white bread and the result tastes delicious.

Mediterranean Bruschetta

Serves 4

INGREDIENTS

1 ciabatta loaf or small stick of French bread	1 plump clove garlic extra virgin olive oil	fresh Parmesan cheese, grated (optional)

1 Slice the bread in half crossways and again lengthwise to give 4 portions.

2 Do not peel the garlic clove, but cut it in half.

3 Barbecue (grill) the bread over hot coals for a few minutes on both sides until golden brown.

4 Rub the garlic, cut side down, all over the toasted surface of the bread.

5 Drizzle the olive oil over the bread and serve hot as an accompaniment.

6 If using Parmesan cheese, sprinkle the cheese over the bread. Return the bread to the barbecue (grill), cut side up, for 1–2 minutes until the cheese just begins to melt. Serve hot.

VARIATION

For a tasty appetizer, serve the bruschetta topped with chopped tomatoes mixed with a few chopped anchovies or olives.

COOK'S TIP

As ready-grated Parmesan quickly loses its pungency and 'bite', it is better to buy small quantities of the cheese in one piece and grate it yourself as needed. Tightly wrapped in cling film (plastic wrap) or foil, it will keep in the refrigerator for several months. Grate it just before using, for maximum flavour.

COOK'S TIP

If you do not peel the garlic the smell will not transfer to your fingers.

Caesar Salad

Serves 6-8

INGREDIENTS

2 thick slices of white bread
2 tbsp sunflower oil
2 rashers streaky bacon

1 clove garlic
1 large cos (romaine) lettuce
50 g/1³/4 oz fresh Parmesan
cheese

DRESSING:
1 small egg
juice of 1 lemon
6 tbsp olive oil
salt and white pepper

---

1 To make the croûtons, remove the crusts from the bread and discard. Cut the bread into small cubes. Heat the oil in a frying pan (skillet) and fry the bread cubes until golden-brown. Drain on absorbent kitchen paper.

2 Remove the rind from the bacon and discard. Chop the bacon and fry until crisp. Drain on absorbent kitchen paper.

3 Cut the garlic in half and rub all around the inside of a serving dish.

This will give the salad just a hint of garlic.

4 Wash the lettuce, tear into bite-size pieces and then place in the serving dish.

5 Using a potato peeler, shave peelings off the Parmesan.

6 To make the dressing, whisk the egg in a small bowl. Gradually whisk in the lemon juice and oil. Season with a little salt and pepper to taste.

7 Pour the salad dressing over the lettuce and toss to coat. Serve sprinkled with the croûtons, bacon and Parmesan shavings.

COOK'S TIP

Pregnant women, children and people with weak immune systems may wish to avoid eating recipes containing raw egg.

Coleslaw

Serves 10–12

INGREDIENTS

150 ml/5 fl oz/²/₃ cup
    mayonnaise
150 ml/5 fl oz/²/₃ cup low-fat
    natural yogurt

dash of Tabasco sauce
1 medium head white cabbage
4 carrots
1 green (bell) pepper

2 tbsp sunflower seeds
salt and pepper

1 To make the dressing, combine the mayonnaise, yogurt, Tabasco sauce and salt and pepper to taste in a small bowl. Leave to chill in the refrigerator until required.

2 Cut the cabbage in half and then into quarters. Remove and discard the tough centre stalk. Shred the cabbage leaves finely. Wash the leaves and dry them thoroughly.

3 Peel the carrot and shred in a food processor. Alternatively, coarsely grate the carrot.

4 Quarter and deseed the (bell) pepper and cut the flesh into thin strips.

5 Combine the vegetables in a large serving bowl and toss. Pour over the dressing and toss until well coated, then chill.

6 Just before serving, place the sunflower seeds on a baking tray and toast them in the oven or under the grill (broiler) until golden brown.

7 Scatter the sunflower seeds over the coleslaw and serve.

COOK'S TIP

You can make coleslaw a few days in advance. To ensure that the sunflower seeds are crispy, add them just before serving.

VARIATION

For a slightly different taste, try the following ingredients in the coleslaw:
raisins, grapes, grated apple, chopped walnuts, cubes of cheese or roasted peanuts.

Green Bean & Carrot Salad

Serves 4

INGREDIENTS

350 g/12 oz green (French) beans	DRESSING:	salt and pepper
225 g/8 oz carrots	2 tbsp extra virgin olive oil	
1 red (bell) pepper	1 tbsp red wine vinegar	
1 red onion	2 tsp sun-dried tomato paste	
	1/4 tsp caster (superfine) sugar	

1 Top and tail the beans and blanch them in boiling water for 4 minutes, until tender. Drain the beans and rinse under cold water until cooled. Drain again.

2 Transfer the beans to a large salad bowl.

3 Peel the carrots and cut them into thin matchsticks, using a mandolin if you have one.

4 Halve and deseed the (bell) pepper and cut the flesh into thin strips.

5 Peel the onion and cut it into thin slices.

6 Add the carrot, (bell) pepper and onion to the beans and toss to mix.

7 To make the dressing, place the oil, wine vinegar, sun-dried tomato paste, sugar and salt and pepper to taste in a screw-top jar and shake well.

8 Pour the dressing over the vegetables and serve immediately or leave to chill in the refrigerator until required.

COOK'S TIP

Use canned beans if fresh ones are unavailable. Rinse off the salty liquid and drain well. There is no need to blanch canned beans.

Spinach & Orange Salad

Serves 4-6

INGREDIENTS

225 g/8 oz baby spinach
  leaves
2 large oranges
1/2 red onion

DRESSING:
3 tbsp extra virgin olive oil
2 tbsp freshly squeezed
  orange juice
2 tsp lemon juice

1 tsp clear honey
1/2 tsp wholegrain mustard
salt and pepper

1 Wash the spinach leaves under cold running water and then dry them thoroughly on absorbent kitchen paper. Remove any tough stalks and tear the larger leaves into smaller pieces.

2 Slice the top and bottom off each orange with a sharp knife, then remove the peel.

3 Carefully slice between the membranes of the orange to remove the individual segments.

4 Using a sharp knife, finely chop the onion.

5 Mix together the salad leaves and orange segments and arrange in a serving dish. Scatter the chopped onion over.

6 To make the dressing, whisk together the olive oil, orange juice, lemon juice, honey, mustard and salt and pepper to taste.

7 Pour the dressing over the salad just before serving. Toss the salad well to coat the leaves with the dressing.

COOK'S TIP

Tear the spinach leaves into bite-sized pieces rather than cutting them because cutting bruises the leaves.

VARIATION

Use a mixture of spinach and watercress leaves, if you prefer a slightly more peppery flavour.

Potato Salad

Serves 4

INGREDIENTS

700 g/1 lb 9 oz tiny new
    potatoes
8 spring onions (scallions)
1 hard-boiled (hard-cooked)
    egg (optional)

250 ml/9 fl oz/1 cup
    mayonnaise
1 tsp paprika
salt and pepper

TO GARNISH:
2 tbsp chives, snipped
pinch of paprika

1 Bring a large pan of lightly salted water to the boil. Add the potatoes to the pan and cook for 10–15 minutes or until they are just tender.

2 Drain the potatoes in a colander and rinse them under cold running water until they are completely cold. Drain them again thoroughly. Transfer the potatoes to a mixing bowl and set aside until required.

3 Using a sharp knife, trim and slice the spring onions (scallions) thinly on the diagonal.

4 Chop the hard-boiled (hard-cooked) egg.

5 Combine the mayonnaise, paprika and salt and pepper to taste in a bowl. Pour the mixture over the potatoes.

6 Add the spring onions (scallions) and egg (if using) to the potatoes and toss together.

7 Transfer the potato salad to a serving bowl, sprinkle with snipped chives and a pinch of paprika. Cover and leave to chill in the refrigerator.

VARIATION

To make a lighter dressing, use a mixture of half mayonnaise and half natural yogurt.

VARIATION

Add cubes of cheese to the potato salad, if liked.

Tabouleh

Serves 4

INGREDIENTS

225 g/8 oz/2 cups cracked
   wheat
225 g/8 oz tomatoes
1 small onion
1/4 cucumber

1/2 red (bell) pepper
4 tbsp chopped, fresh parsley
3 tbsp chopped, fresh mint
2 tbsp pine nuts
4 tbsp lemon juice

4 tbsp extra virgin olive oil
2 cloves garlic, crushed
salt and pepper

---

1 Place the cracked wheat in a large bowl and cover with plenty of boiling water. Leave to stand for about 30 minutes or until the grains are tender and have swelled in size.

2 Drain the wheat through a large sieve. Press down with a plate in order to remove as much water as possible. Transfer the wheat to a large bowl.

3 Cut the tomatoes in half, scoop out the seeds and discard them. Chop the flesh into fine dice. Using a sharp knife, finely chop the onion.

4 Scoop out the seeds from the cucumber and discard them. Finely dice the cucumber flesh.

5 Deseed the (bell) peppers and chop the flesh. Add the prepared vegetables to the wheat with the herbs and pine nuts. Toss until mixed.

6 Mix together the lemon juice oil, garlic and salt and pepper to taste in a small bowl.

7 Pour the mixture over the wheat and vegetables and toss together. Leave to chill in the refrigerator until required.

COOK'S TIP

This salad is best made a few hours before it is required to allow time for the flavours to develop and blend together. It can even be made a few days ahead, if wished.

Hot Lentil Salad
with Balsamic Dressing

Serves 6–8

INGREDIENTS

175 g/6 oz Puy lentils, cooked
4 tbsp olive oil
1 small onion, sliced
4 sticks celery, sliced
2 cloves garlic, crushed
2 courgettes (zucchini),
    trimmed and diced

125 g/4¹/₂ oz green (French)
    beans, trimmed and cut
    into short lengths
¹/₂ red (bell) pepper, deseeded
    and diced
¹/₂ yellow (bell) pepper,
    deseeded and diced

1 tsp Dijon mustard
1 tbsp balsamic vinegar
salt and pepper

1 Place the lentils in a large mixing or serving bowl. The lentils can still be warm, if wished.

2 Heat the oil in a pan and fry the onion and celery for 2–3 minutes until softened.

3 Stir the garlic, courgettes (zucchini) and green (French) beans into the pan and cook for a further 2 minutes.

4 Add the (bell) peppers to the pan and cook for 1 minute.

5 Stir the mustard and the balsamic vinegar into the pan and mix until warm and well combined.

6 Pour the warm mixture over the lentils and toss together to mix well. Season with salt and pepper to taste and serve immediately.

COOK'S TIP

To cook the lentils, rinse them well and place in a large saucepan. Cover with plenty of cold water and bring to the boil. Boil rapidly for 10 minutes, then reduce the heat and simmer for 35 minutes until the lentils are tender. Drain well.

Italian Mozzarella Salad

Serves 6

INGREDIENTS

200 g/7 oz baby spinach
125 g/4 1/2 oz watercress
125 g/4 1/2 oz Mozzarella
cheese

225 g/8 oz cherry tomatoes
2 tsp balsamic vinegar
1 1/2 tbsp extra virgin olive oil

salt and freshly ground black
pepper

1 Wash the spinach and watercress and drain thoroughly on absorbent kitchen paper. Remove any tough stalks. Place the spinach and watercress leaves in a serving dish.

2 Cut the Mozzarella into small pieces and scatter them over the spinach and watercress leaves.

3 Cut the cherry tomatoes in half and scatter them over the salad.

4 Sprinkle over the balsamic vinegar and oil, and season with salt and pepper to taste. Toss the mixture together to coat the leaves. Serve at once or leave to chill in the refrigerator until required.

VARIATION

Include Feta or Halloumi cheese instead of Mozzarella for a change, and use sherry vinegar instead of balsamic vinegar, if preferred.

COOK'S TIP

Mozzarella is a highly popular cheese. It is a soft, fresh cheese with a piquant flavour, traditionally made from water buffalo's milk. It is usually sold surrounded by whey to keep it moist. Buffalo milk is now scarce, and so nowadays this cheese is often made with cow's milk. Mozzarella combines well with tomatoes, and this combination is now a classic.

Artichoke & Parma Ham (Prosciutto) Salad

Serves 4

INGREDIENTS

275 g/9^1/$_2$ oz can artichoke
    hearts in oil, drained
4 small tomatoes
25 g/1 oz sun-dried tomatoes
    in oil
40 g/1^1/$_2$ oz Parma ham
    (prosciutto)

25 g/1 oz pitted black olives,
    halved
few basil leaves

DRESSING:
3 tbsp olive oil
1 tbsp white wine vinegar

1 clove garlic, crushed
^{1}/$_2$ tsp mild mustard
1 tsp clear honey
salt and pepper

1 Make sure the artichokes hearts are thoroughly drained, then cut them into quarters and place in a bowl until required.

2 Cut each fresh tomato into wedges. Slice the sun-dried tomatoes into thin strips. Cut the Parma ham (prosciutto) into thin strips and add to the bowl with the tomatoes and olive halves.

3 Keeping a few basil leaves whole for garnishing, tear the remainder of the leaves into small pieces and add to the bowl containing the other salad ingredients.

4 Put the oil, wine vinegar, garlic, mustard, honey and salt and pepper to taste in a screw-top jar and shake vigorously until well blended.

5 Pour the dressing over the salad and toss.

6 Serve the salad garnished with a few whole basil leaves.

COOK'S TIP

Use bottled artichokes in oil as they have a better flavour. Rinse canned artichokes to remove the salty liquid.

Pear & Roquefort Salad

Serves 4

INGREDIENTS

50 g/1³/₄ oz Roquefort cheese
150 ml/5 fl oz/²/₃ cup low-fat
    natural yogurt
2 tbsp snipped chives

few leaves of lollo rosso
few leaves of radiccio
few leaves of lamb's lettuce
    (corn salad)

2 ripe pears
pepper
whole chives, to garnish

1 Place the cheese in a bowl and mash with a fork. Gradually blend the yogurt into the cheese to make a smooth dressing. Add the chives and season with a little pepper according to taste.

2 Tear the lollo rosso, radiccio and lamb's lettuce leaves into manageable pieces. Arrange the salad leaves on a serving platter or on individual serving plates.

3 Quarter and core the pears and then cut them into slices.

4 Arrange the pear slices over the salad leaves.

5 Drizzle the dressing over the pears and garnish with a few whole chives. Serve at once.

COOK'S TIP

Arrange the Pear and Roquefort Salad on individual plates for an attractive starter, or on one large serving platter for a side salad.

COOK'S TIP

Look out for bags of mixed salad leaves as these are generally more economical than buying lots of different leaves separately. If you are using leaves that have not been prewashed, rinse them well and dry them thoroughly on absorbent paper kitchen towels or in a salad spinner. Alternatively, wrap the leaves in a clean tea towel (dish cloth) and shake dry.

Pasta Salad with Basil Vinaigrette

Serves 4

INGREDIENTS

225 g/8 oz fusilli (pasta spirals)
4 tomatoes
50 g/1³/4 oz black olives
25 g/1 oz sun-dried tomatoes in oil
2 tbsp pine nuts

2 tbsp grated Parmesan cheese
fresh basil, to garnish

VINAIGRETTE:
15 g/¹/2 oz basil leaves
1 clove garlic

2 tbsp grated Parmesan cheese
4 tbsp extra virgin olive oil
2 tbsp lemon juice
salt and pepper

1 Cook the pasta in lightly salted boiling water for 10–12 minutes until just tender, or according to the instructions on the packet. Drain the pasta, rinse under cold water, then drain again thoroughly. Place the pasta in a large bowl.

2 To make the vinaigrette, place the basil leaves, garlic, cheese, oil and lemon juice in a food processor. Season with salt and pepper to taste. Process until the leaves are well chopped and the ingredients are combined. Alternatively, finely chop the basil leaves by hand and combine with the other vinaigrette ingredients. Pour the vinaigrette over the pasta and toss to coat.

3 Cut the tomatoes into wedges. Pit and halve the olives. Slice the sun-dried tomatoes. Toast the pine nuts on a baking tray under the grill (broiler) until golden.

4 Add the tomatoes (fresh and sun-dried) and the olives to the pasta and mix until combined.

5 Transfer the pasta to a serving dish, scatter over the Parmesan and pine nuts and garnish with a few basil leaves.

Mango & Wild Rice Salad

Serves 6

INGREDIENTS

75 g/2³/4 oz/¹/2 cup wild rice
150 g/5¹/2 oz/1 cup Basmati
rice
3 tbsp hazelnut oil
1 tbsp sherry vinegar
1 ripe mango

3 sticks celery
75 g/2³/4 oz ready-to-eat
dried apricots, chopped
75 g/2³/4 oz flaked (slivered)
almonds, toasted

2 tbsp chopped, fresh
coriander (cilantro) or mint
salt and pepper
sprigs of fresh coriander
(cilantro) or mint, to
garnish

1 Cook the rice in separate saucepans in lightly salted boiling water. Cook the wild rice for 45–50 minutes and the Basmati rice for 10–12 minutes. Drain, rinse well and drain again. Place in a large bowl.

2 Mix the oil, vinegar and seasoning together. Pour the mixture over the rice and toss well.

3 Cut the mango in half lengthwise, as close to the stone as possible.

Remove and discard the stone.

4 Peel the skin from the mango and cut the flesh into slices.

5 Slice the celery thinly and add to the cooled rice with the mango, apricots, almonds and chopped herbs. Toss together and transfer to a serving dish. Garnish with sprigs of fresh herbs.

COOK'S TIP

To toast almonds, place them on a baking sheet in a preheated oven 180°C/350°F/Gas Mark 4 for 5–10 minutes. Alternatively, toast them under the grill (broiler), turning frequently and keeping a close eye on them because they will quickly burn.

Mixed Bean Salad

Serves 6-8

INGREDIENTS

400 g/14 oz can flageolet
(small navy) beans, drained
400 g/14 oz can red kidney
beans, drained
400 g/14 oz can butter beans,
drained

1 small red onion, thinly sliced
175 g/6 oz dwarf green beans,
topped and tailed
1 red (bell) pepper, halved and
deseeded

DRESSING:
4 tbsp olive oil
2 tbsp sherry vinegar
2 tbsp lemon juice
1 tsp light muscovado sugar
1 tsp chilli sauce (optional)

1 Put the canned beans in a large mixing bowl. Add the sliced onion and mix together.

2 Cut the dwarf green beans in half and cook in lightly salted boiling water for about 8 minutes until just tender. Refresh under cold water and drain again. Add to the mixed beans and onions.

3 Place the (bell) pepper halves, cut side down, on a grill (broiler) rack and cook until the skin

blackens and chars. Leave to cool slightly then pop them into a plastic bag for about 10 minutes. Peel away the skin from the (bell) peppers and discard. Chop the (bell) pepper flesh and add to the beans.

4 To make the dressing, place the oil, sherry vinegar, lemon juice, sugar and chilli sauce (if using) in a screw-top jar and shake vigorously.

5 Pour the dressing over the mixed bean salad

and toss well. Leave to chill in the refrigerator until required.

VARIATION

You can use any combination of beans in this salad. For a distinctive flavour, add 1 teaspoon of curry paste instead of the chilli sauce.

Mediterranean (Bell) Pepper Salad

Serves 4

INGREDIENTS

2 red (bell) peppers, halved and deseeded	1 onion, cut into wedges	50 g/1¾ oz anchovy fillets, chopped
2 yellow (bell) peppers, halved and deseeded	2 large courgettes (zucchini), sliced	25 g/1 oz pitted black olives, quartered
3 tbsp extra virgin olive oil	2 garlic cloves, sliced	fresh basil leaves
	1 tbsp balsamic vinegar	

1 Place the (bell) pepper halves, cut side down, on a grill (broiler) pan and cook until the skin blackens and chars. Leave to cool slightly then pop them into a plastic bag for about 10 minutes.

2 Peel away the skin from the (bell) peppers and discard. Cut the flesh into thick strips.

3 Heat the oil in a large frying pan (skillet), add the onion and cook gently for 10 minutes or until softened. Add the

courgette (zucchini) slices, garlic and (bell) pepper strips to the pan and cook, stirring occasionally, for a further 10 minutes.

4 Add the vinegar, anchovies and olives to the pan. Season to taste. Mix well and leave to cool.

5 Reserve a few basil leaves for garnishing, then tear the remainder into small pieces. Stir them into the salad.

6 Transfer the salad to a serving dish and

garnish with a few whole basil leaves.

COOK'S TIP

Balsamic vinegar is made in and around Modena in Italy. Its rich, mellow flavour is perfect for Mediterranean-style salads, but if it is unavailable, use sherry vinegar or white wine vinegar instead.

Desserts

Don't forget the dessert – it can be cooked on the barbecue (grill), too. Although desserts are not the most important part of a barbecue (grill) spread, they are always fun to cook and most can be prepared in advance and left above the cooling coals to cook to perfection while you tuck into the main course.

Fruit is always a good choice because it contrasts so well with the often rich and filling main courses. Try croissants filled with chocolate and raspberries or panettone topped with marscapone cheese.

Have plenty of ice cream as a stand-by. It's popular with the children and is delicious served with barbecued (grilled) fruits on a hot summer day. Thick natural yogurt or single (light) cream are also ideal accompaniments. If you don't want a hot dessert, prepare a simple fruit salad.

For a quick sweet treat thread marshmallows on to skewers and hold them above the warm coals until just softened. Alternatively, try threading cubes of teacake on to a skewer, toast until golden and serve with a little maple syrup.

Barbecued (Grilled) Baked Apples

Serves 4

INGREDIENTS

4 medium cooking apples
25 g/1 oz walnuts, chopped
25 g/1 oz ground almonds
25 g/1 oz light muscovado
  sugar

25 g/1 oz cherries, chopped
25 g/1 oz stem ginger,
  chopped
1 tbsp amaretto (almond-
  flavoured liqueur) (optional)

50 g/1³/4 oz butter
single (light) cream or natural
  yogurt, to serve

1 Core the apples and using a knife, score each one around the middle to prevent the apple skins from splitting during barbecueing (grilling).

2 To make the filling, mix together the walnuts, almonds, sugar, cherries, ginger and amaretto (almond-flavoured liqueur), if using, in a small bowl.

3 Spoon the filling mixture into each apple, pushing it down into the hollowed-out core.

Mound a little of the filling on top of each apple.

4 Place each apple on a large square of double thickness kitchen foil and generously dot all over with the butter. Wrap up the foil so that the apple is completely enclosed.

5 Barbecue (grill) the foil parcels containing the apples over hot coals for 25–30 minutes or until tender.

6 Transfer the apples to warm, individual

serving plates. Serve with lashings of whipped single (light) cream or thick natural yogurt.

COOK'S TIP

If the coals are dying down, place the kitchen foil parcels directly on to the coals, raking them up around the apples. Barbecue (grill) for 25–30 minutes and serve with the cream or yogurt.

Fruity Skewers with Chocolate Dipping Sauce

Serves 4

INGREDIENTS

Selection of fruit (choose from oranges, bananas, strawberries, pineapple chunks (fresh or canned), apricots (fresh or canned), dessert (eating) apples, pears, kiwi fruit)

1 tbsp lemon juice

CHOCOLATE SAUCE:
50 g/1^3/4 oz butter
50 g/1^3/4 oz dark chocolate, broken into small cubes
^{1}/2 tbsp cocoa powder

2 tbsp golden syrup

BASTE:
4 tbsp clear honey
grated rind and juice of ^{1}/2 orange

1 To make the chocolate sauce, place the butter, chocolate, cocoa powder and golden syrup in a small pan. Heat gently on a stove or at the side of the barbecue (grill), stirring continuously, until all of the ingredients have melted and are well combined.

2 To prepare the fruit, peel and core if necessary, then cut into large, bite-size pieces or wedges as appropriate. Dip apples, pears and bananas in lemon juice to prevent discoloration. Thread the fruit on to skewers.

3 To make the baste, mix the honey, orange juice and rind, heat gently and brush over the fruit.

4 Barbecue (grill) the fruit skewers over warm coals for 5–10 minutes until hot. Serve with the chocolate dipping sauce.

COOK'S TIP

If the coals are too hot raise the rack so that it is about 15 cm/6 inches above the coals or spread out the coals a little to reduce the heat. Do not assemble the skewers more than 1-2 hours before they are required.

Toffee Fruit Kebabs (Kabobs)

Serves 4

INGREDIENTS

2 dessert (eating) apples
2 firm pears, cored and cut
    into wedges
juice of 1/2 lemon

25 g/1 oz light muscovado
    sugar
1/4 tsp ground allspice
25 g/1 oz unsalted butter,
    melted

SAUCE:
125 g/41/2 oz butter
100 g/31/2 oz light
    muscovado sugar
6 tbsp double (heavy) cream

1 Core the apples and cut them into wedges. Toss the apple and pears in the lemon juice to prevent any discoloration.

2 Mix the sugar and allspice together and sprinkle over the fruit.

3 Thread the fruit pieces on to skewers.

4 To make the toffee sauce, place the butter and sugar in a saucepan and heat, stirring gently, until the butter has melted and the sugar has dissolved.

5 Add the cream to the pan and bring to the boil. Boil for 1–2 minutes, then set aside.

6 Meanwhile, place the fruit kebabs (kabobs) over hot coals and barbecue (grill) for about 5 minutes, turning and basting frequently with the melted butter, until the fruit is just tender.

7 Transfer the fruit kebabs (kabobs) to warm serving plates and serve with the slightly cooled toffee sauce.

COOK'S TIP

Firm apples that will keep their shape are needed for this dish – varieties such as Golden Delicious, Granny Smith and Braeburn are a good choice. Soft apples and pears will become mushy as they cook.

VARIATION

Sprinkle the fruit kebabs (kabobs) with chopped walnuts or pecan nuts before serving, if you wish.

Chocolate & Raspberry Croissants

Serves 4

INGREDIENTS

4 butter croissants	75 g/2¾ oz dark chocolate	oil, for greasing
4 tsp raspberry preserve	125 g/ 4½ oz raspberries	

1 Slice the croissants in half. Spread the bottom half of each croissant with 1 teaspoon of the raspberry preserve.

2 Grate or finely chop the chocolate and sprinkle over the raspberry preserve.

3 Lightly grease 4 sheets of kitchen foil, brushing with a little oil.

4 Divide the raspberries among the croissants and replace the top half of each croissant. Place each croissant on to a sheet of foil, wrapping the foil to enclose it completely.

5 Place the rack 15 cm/6 inches above hot coals. Transfer the croissants to the rack and leave them to heat through for 10–15 minutes or until the chocolate just begins to melt.

6 Remove the foil and transfer the croissants to individual serving plates. Serve hot.

VARIATION

You could also use milk chocolate or a mixture of milk and dark chocolate for this dish.

VARIATION

For a delicious chocolate and strawberry filling for the croissants, use sliced strawberries and strawberry preserve instead of the raspberries.

COOK'S TIP

Use the best quality fruit preserve you can find. Better still, use homemade jams and preserves.

Baked Bananas

Serves 4

INGREDIENTS

4 bananas	ORANGE-FLAVOURED CREAM:	2 tbsp orange-flavoured
2 passion fruit	150 ml/5 fl oz/ ²⁄₃ cup double	liqueur
4 tbsp orange juice	(heavy) cream	
4 tbsp orange-flavoured	3 tbsp icing (confectioners')	
liqueur	sugar	

1 Peel the bananas and place each one on to a sheet of kitchen foil.

2 Cut the passion fruit in half and squeeze the juice of each half over each banana. Spoon over the orange juice and liqueur.

3 Fold the kitchen foil over the top of the bananas to enclose the bananas completely.

4 Barbecue (grill) the bananas over hot coals for about 10 minutes or until they are just tender.

5 To make the orange-flavoured cream, pour the double (heavy) cream into a mixing bowl and sprinkle over the icing (confectioners') sugar. Whisk the mixture until it is standing in soft peaks. Carefully fold in the orange-flavoured liqueur and leave to chill in the refrigerator until required.

6 Transfer the foil parcel containing the bananas to warm, individual serving plates. Open out the foil parcels at the table and then serve the bananas immediately with the orange-flavoured cream.

VARIATION

Leave the bananas in their skins for a really quick dessert. Split the banana skins and pop in 1–2 cubes of chocolate. Wrap the bananas in kitchen foil and barbecue (grill) for 10 minutes, or until the chocolate just melts.

Panettone with Mascarpone & Strawberries

Serves 4

INGREDIENTS

225 g/8 oz strawberries
25 g/1 oz caster (superfine)
sugar

6 tbsp Marsala wine
1/2 tsp ground cinnamon

4 slices panettone
4 tbsp mascarpone cheese

1 Hull and slice the strawberries and place them in a bowl. Add the sugar, Marsala and cinnamon to the strawberries.

2 Toss the strawberries in the sugar and cinnamon mixture until they are well coated. Leave to chill in the refrigerator for at least 30 minutes.

3 When ready to serve, transfer the slices of panettone to a rack set over medium hot coals. Barbecue (grill) the

panettone for about 1 minute on each side or until golden brown.

4 Remove the panettone from the barbecue (grill) and transfer to serving plates. Top the panettone with the mascarpone cheese and the marinated strawberries. Serve immediately.

VARIATION

Spread mascarpone cheese on to teacakes that have been toasted on the barbecue (grill).

COOK'S TIP

Mascarpone is an Italian soft cheese with a rich, creamy texture, which tastes like very thick cream. It will melt into the panettone, making it quite delicious. If mascarpone is unavailable, clotted cream would be a good alternative.

Pina Colada Pineapple

Serves 4

INGREDIENTS

1 small pineapple
50 g/1³/₄ oz unsalted butter
25 g/1 oz light muscovado
  sugar

50 g/1³/₄ oz fresh coconut,
  grated
2 tbsp coconut-flavoured
  liqueur or rum

1 Using a very sharp knife, cut the pineapple into quarters and then remove the tough core from the centre, leaving the leaves attached.

2 Cut the pineapple flesh away from the skin. Make horizontal cuts across the flesh of the pineapple quarters.

3 Place the butter in a pan and heat gently until melted, stirring continuously. Brush the melted butter over the pineapple and sprinkle with the sugar.

4 Cover the pineapple leaves with kitchen foil in order to prevent them from burning and transfer them to a rack set over hot coals.

5 Barbecue (grill) the pineapple for about 10 minutes.

6 Sprinkle the coconut over the pineapple and barbecue (grill), cut side up, for a further 5–10 minutes or until the pineapple is piping hot.

7 Transfer the pineapple to serving plates and remove the foil from the leaves. Spoon a little coconut-flavoured liqueur or rum over the pineapple and serve immediately.

COOK'S TIP

Fresh coconut has the best flavour for this dish. If you prefer, however, you can use desiccated (shredded) coconut.

Stuffed Pears with Mincemeat

Serves 4

INGREDIENTS

4 firm pears
1 tsp lemon juice
2 tbsp mincemeat

5 tbsp cake crumbs or 4
amaretti biscuits, crushed

15 g/$^{1}/_{2}$ oz butter
ice cream, to serve

1 Using a sharp knife, cut the pears in half. Using a teaspoon, scoop out the core and discard.

2 Brush the cut surface of each of the pear halves with a little lemon juice to prevent discoloration.

3 Mix together the mincemeat and cake crumbs or crushed amaretti biscuits.

4 Divide the mixture among the pear halves, spooning it into a mound where the core has been removed.

5 Place 2 pear halves on a large square of double thickness kitchen foil and generously dot all over with the butter.

6 Wrap up the foil around the pears so that they are enclosed.

7 Transfer the foil parcels to a rack set over hot coals. Barbecue (grill) for 25–30 minutes or until the pears are hot and just tender.

8 Transfer the pears to individual serving plates. Serve with 2 scoops of ice cream per serving.

VARIATION

Use mincemeat to stuff apples instead of pears and bake them on the barbecue (grill) in the same way.

COOK'S TIP

If the coals are dying down, place the kitchen foil parcels directly on to the coals and barbecue (grill) for 25–30 minutes.

Peaches with
Creamy Mascarpone Filling

Serves 4

INGREDIENTS

4 peaches
175 g/6 oz mascarpone cheese

40 g/1 1/2 oz pecan or walnuts,
chopped

1 tsp sunflower oil
4 tbsp maple syrup

1 Cut the peaches in half and remove the stones. If you are preparing this recipe in advance, press the peach halves together again and wrap them in cling film (plastic wrap) until required.

2 Mix the mascarpone and pecan or walnuts together in a small bowl until well combined. Leave to chill in the refrigerator until required.

3 To serve, brush the peaches with a little oil and place on a rack set over medium hot coals.

Barbecue (grill) the peach halves for 5–10 minutes, turning once, until hot.

4 Transfer the peach halves to a dish and top with the mascarpone and nut mixture.

5 Drizzle the maple syrup over the peaches and mascarpone filling and serve at once.

COOK'S TIP

Mascarpone cheese is high in fat; you can use thick natural yogurt instead.

VARIATION

You can use nectarines instead of peaches for this recipe, if you prefer. Remember to choose ripe but fairly firm fruit which won't go soft and mushy when it is barbecued (grilled). Prepare the nectarines in the same way as the peaches and barbecue (grill) for 5–10 minutes.

Exotic Fruity Parcels

Serves 4

INGREDIENTS

1 pawpaw (papaya)
1 mango
1 star fruit

1 tbsp grenadine
3 tbsp orange juice

single (light) cream or natural
yogurt, to serve

1 Cut the pawpaw (papaya) in half, scoop out the seeds and discard them. Peel the pawpaw (papaya) and cut the flesh into thick slices.

2 Prepare the mango by cutting it lengthwise in half either side of the central stone.

3 Score each mango half in a criss-cross pattern. Push each mango half inside out to separate the cubes and cut them away from the peel.

4 Using a sharp knife, slice the star fruit.

5 Place all of the fruit in a bowl and mix.

6 Mix the grenadine and orange juice together and pour over the fruit. Leave to marinate for at least 30 minutes.

7 Divide the fruit among 4 double thickness squares of kitchen foil and gather up the edges to form a parcel that encloses the fruit.

8 Place the foil parcel on a rack set over warm coals and barbecue (grill) the fruit for about 15–20 minutes.

9 Serve the fruit in the parcel, with single (light) cream or yogurt.

COOK'S TIP

Grenadine is a sweet syrup made from pomegranates. If you prefer you could use pomegranate juice instead of the grenadine for this recipe. To extract the juice, cut the pomegranate in half and squeeze gently with a lemon squeezer – do not press too hard or the juice may become bitter.

Index

Apples, barbecued (grilled) baked 236
artichoke & Parma ham salad 222
aubergine (eggplant): aubergine &
    mozzarella sandwiches 186
    char-grilled aubergine 188
avocado salsa 102

Bacon & scallop skewers 40
bananas, baked 244
beans: mixed bean salad 230
    vegetarian sausages 182
beef: barbecue steaks with red
    onion marmalade 104
    beef teriyaki 98
    beef tomato & olive kebabs 108
    beef toppers 96
    boozy beef steaks 100
    meatball brochettes 112
    Mexican steaks with avocado
    salsa 102
    steak & kidney kebabs 166
    surf & turf kebabs 106
    with wild mushrooms 110
blackened fish 10
bread, garlic 202
bream, char-grilled 18
bruschetta, Mediterranean 204

Caesar salad 206
Cajun spicy chicken 60
Caribbean pork 144
Caribbean prawns (shrimp) 44
cheese: aubergine (eggplant) &
    mozzarella sandwiches 186
    Italian mozzarella salad 220
chicken: Cajun spicy chicken 60
    chicken satay 68
    chicken skewers with lemon
    & coriander (cilantro) 66
    chicken skewers with red
    (bell) pepper sauce 74
    chicken tikka 56
    favourite barbecued (grilled)
    chicken 52
    Indian charred chicken 58
    jerk chicken 50
    Maryland chicken kebabs 76
    sesame chicken brochettes
    with cranberry sauce 72
    spatchcock baby chicken with
    garlic & herbs 62
    sticky drumsticks 54
    sweet maple chicken 64
    Thai-style chicken skewers 70
chocolate & raspberry croissants 242
cod, Indonesian-style spicy 8
coleslaw 208
corn-on-the-cob 198
cracked wheat: tabouleh 216
croissants, chocolate & raspberry 242

Desserts 235–54
duck: barbecued (grilled) duckling 90

citrus duckling skewers 64
glazed duckling with pineapple
    salsa 92
sesame orange duckling 68

Fish & seafood 7–46
fruit: exotic fruity kebabs 254
    fruity skewers with chocolate
    dipping sauce 238
    toffee fruit kebabs 240

Garlic bread 202
green bean & carrot salad 210

Ham: ham & pineapple kebabs 156
    steaks with spicy apple rings 146
herrings: barbecued with lemon 36
    with orange tarragon stuffing 42

Indian charred chicken 58
Indian kofta 138
Indonesian-style spicy cod 8
Italian mozzarella salad 220

Japanese-style char-grilled plaice 24
jerk chicken 50

Kibbeh 122

Lamb: barbecued (grilled) ribs 124
    burgers with mint & pine nuts 116
    butterfly chops with
    redcurrant glaze 118
    butterfly lamb with balsamic
    vinegar & mint 126
    cutlets with rosemary 134
    Indian kofta 138
    kibbeh 122
    Moroccan kebabs 130
    noisettes with tomato salsa 142
    red wine lamb skewers 128
    shish kebabs 132
    sweet lamb fillet 140
    with a spice crust 120
    with mango & chilli 136
lentil salad with balsamic dressing 218
liver: liver & onion kebabs 170
    sherried chicken liver brochettes 84

Mackerel: apricot char-grilled
    mackerel 28
    with lime & coriander (cilantro) 30
mango & wild rice salad 228
Maryland chicken kebabs 76
meat 95–170
meatball brochettes 112
Mediterranean (bell) pepper salad 232
Mediterranean bruschetta 204
Mediterranean-style sardines 32
Mexican steaks with avocado salsa 102
mixed grill skewers 168
monkfish: skewers with coconut &
    coriander (cilantro) 14
    skewers with courgettes
    (zucchini) & lemon 12
Moroccan lamb kebabs 130
mushrooms, stuffed 196

Panettone with mascarpone &
    strawberries 246
pasta salad with basil vinaigrette 226
peaches with creamy mascarpone
    filling 252
pears: pear & Roquefort salad 224
    stuffed with mincemeat 250
pepper (bell) salad, Mediterranean 232
pineapple: Pina Colada 248
plaice (flounder), Japanese-style
    char-grilled 24
pork: Caribbean pork 144
    fruity pork skewers 152
    honey-glazed pork 158
    pork & apple skewers with
    mustard 148
    pork & sage kebabs 164
    ribs with plum sauce 150
    spicy pork ribs 154
    tangy pork fillet 162
potatoes: barbecued (grilled) garlic
    potato wedges 180
    crispy potato skins 176
    potato salad 214
poultry 47–92
prawns (shrimp): Caribbean prawns 44
    herb & garlic prawns 46
pumpkin parcels with chilli & lime 200

Rice burgers, nutty 184

Salads 206–32
salmon: salmon brochettes 22
    salmon yakitori 20
sardines: Mediterranean-style 32
    with olives & tomatoes 38
sausages: vegetarian 182
    with barbecue sauce 160
scallops: bacon & scallop skewers 40
sea bream, char-grilled 18
shish kebabs 132
smoked cod: smoky fish skewers 26
spinach & orange salad 212
steak & kidney kebabs 166
surf & turf kebabs 106
sweet potato slices, spicy 178

Tabouleh 216
Thai-style chicken skewers 70
toffee fruit kebabs 240
tofu (bean curd) skewers, marinated 174
tomatoes, stuffed 190
trout, nutty stuffed 34
tuna steaks, charred 16
turkey: char-grilled turkey with
    cheesy pockets 80
    spicy turkey & sausage kebabs 82
    turkey steaks with redcurrant
    glaze 78

Vegetables 173–200
    char-grilled mixed vegetables 194
    colourful vegetable kebabs 192
vegetarian sausages 182
venison steaks, char-grilled 114

Index compiled by Hilary Bird.